Projects for Creative Woodcarving

D1288875

Projects
for
Creative Woodcarving

Ian Norbury

LINDEN PUBLISHING COMPANY
FRESNO, CA.

Library of Congress Cataloging-in-Publication Data

Norbury, Ian.
    Projects for creative woodcarving / Ian Norbury. -- Rev. ed.
      p. cm.
    ISBN 0–941936–30–9 :
    1. Wood-carving.   I. Title.
TT199.7.N67   1994   94–32689
731.4'62–dc20   CIP

 23456789

Published 1995 by
Linden Publishing Company Inc.
336 W. Bedford, Suite 107
Fresno, CA 93711

Phone 1–800–345–4447

Printed in the United States of America

For Alan, Jayne and James

Acknowledgements

I would like to acknowledge Eric Penning, Jayne Norbury, Michael Price, Dave Johnson and James Norbury for their patience as models; Ken and Pat Ilott for their photographic expertise; Mr & Mrs G. Thompson, Mr & Mrs G. Wyse, Mr & Mrs J. W. Beaver, Mr & Mrs R. G. Vincent, Mr & Mrs R. I. Herbert, Mrs C. Stephenson, Mr. R. Woolridge, Mr & Mrs G. Hancox, Mr & Mrs B. J. Davies, Mr & Mrs D. Johnson, Mr M. Bradley, Mr & Mrs H. B. Sands, Mr & Mrs A. N. Dee, Mr & Mrs P. K. Collier, Mr D. C. C. Wilson, Mr & Mrs R. Jackson, Mr & Mrs A. R. Bewes, Mr & Mrs B. Chanin, Mr & Mrs D. Wearing, Mr & Mrs C. A. Muller, Mr & Mrs J. Rood, Mr & Mrs N. S. Parrack, Mr & Mrs G. Derrett, Mr & Mrs E. R. Penning, Mrs D. Bradwell, Mr & Mrs K. Hamer, Mrs J. Henbest, Mrs A. Bence, Mr W. Cox-Kuhn, Dr. & Mrs N. Mayne, Mr & Mrs R. Vanden Bosch, Mr & Mrs M. Winlow, Mr & Mrs J. Storer, and Mr & Mrs P. A. Ward for permitting their sculptures to be illustrated.

Contents

INTRODUCTION

There are those who love to carve wood and those who love to produce woodcarvings. I am one of the latter. I am not particularly taken with cutting wood although it can be pleasurable and satisfying; for me the objective is a sculpture. In this book I have tried to satisfy both types of carver with the projects ranging from simple shapes that are relaxing to carve and give full rein to the choice of wood and interpretation of its potential, to subtler, more complex pieces requiring considerable technical expertise and aesthetic judgement, where the material is subordinate to the form.

We live in a world dominated by flat surfaces and pictorial images. Television and photography have reduced the vastness of space to a coloured picture a few inches across, and real experience to an hour sat in front of a little box. Things, places and people we have never seen, touched, heard or smelt are more familiar than our own home town. The picture represents the real world from the day we sit on our mother's knee and she says "This is a lion"; the fact is, as we all soon understand, it is not a lion, it is a picture of a lion, and the danger for the sculptor is that reality may never be encountered.

Many artists and sculptors virtually never leave the studio. I have talked to carvers to whom the idea of actually going out and looking at the real live object they are trying to carve, has never occurred. I have certainly been guilty of this and doubtless will continue to be so. The trouble is not so much that you must see the real thing, it is rather that our two-dimensional view of the world has closed our eyes to shape and form; numbed our hands to textures and contours.

If you are shown an apple and asked to describe it, would you say it is green and red, or would you assess its weight? If shown a coin would you say it was round or cylindrical? This may seem fatuous but it is the biggest obstacle to be overcome by the sculptor. We recognise objects by shape not by form, and if you are to reproduce a three-dimensional object, you must know its form, not merely its profile, its colour and light and shade. So, it is necessary for the woodcarver to develop a new way of looking. With experience of carving this will come; when you look at a face you will look at it more as a shape to be carved and less as a physical appearance of a personality.

The profile drawings given in this book are those that were used to bandsaw the carving block, and the carving should be continued using knowledge of the forms gained by observation from life, backed up by photographs, (I take as many detailed photos myself as I can manage); drawings, studies from books and studies of other sculptures and, when necessary, clay models. Most of all, sculpture is all subject to intuition, interpretation and personal preference. The original concepts may well come from books, television, photographs or real life and the illustrations in the book are a true record of this.

*   *   *

The projects here are aimed at a variety of skill levels and I believe there are examples to suit all abilities and most tastes. Talking to other carvers has taught me that many lack inspiration regarding subject matter, or skill to prepare drawings of a subject. Obviously, there is a limit to the number of subjects in such a book and I have reduced that limit more by grouping the projects into types. My intention is that by including half a dozen or so related projects, reference material and technical information overlaps, except in obvious cases, and any one of the projects may be completed using photos or research notes in a combined way, along with your own research. In fact, I would strongly recommend that the whole book be read before starting on any carving.

Although all the material used in this book is available to copy, I hope that the reader will adapt the subjects to their own individual requirements and tastes rather than slavishly copying them. Use them as a springboard for your own ideas, then draw on your own experience and memory.

The squares on the profile drawing are an aid to copying them, not an indication of size, although most of them are 1″ (25mm) square. There seems little point in even suggesting sizes for other carvers with different needs and different supplies of timber. The tools I have used are those I use in the normal course of work. I do not have an enormous collection of chisels, and, in fact, frequently reduce the number rather than increase it. There are, undoubtedly, tools you can do without, but not many – enough is enough, but enough is necessary.

This book is one of design ideas, therefore a step-by-step approach to individual projects has not been given. It follows naturally from my earlier book *Techniques of Creative Woodcarving* which does show the stages of carving for twelve separate progressively difficult subjects. Here, in this introduction, the portrait head outlines what I would call the basic steps in the creation of a woodcarving. It applies to a great deal of figure carving where the techniques stem from a basic bandsawn shape. You will find the underlying principles of this piece relevant to practically all the work shown.

In the projects, along with other points which I consider interesting or significant, I have pointed out aspects of technique which are radically at variance with those outlined in the following child's portrait head.

Portrait head

1 The front and side profiles are drawn on the block of wood; great care is taken to ensure that they are perfectly level. Any innaccuracy would have disastrous results in the next stage.
2 The profiles are now bandsawn. The front view of the head is cut out first. The waste, with the side view drawn on one piece, is then pinned or taped back in position and the side profile bandsawn. The bandsawn block is recognisably a head. The centreline and eyeline are drawn in.
3 The main waste areas can now be cut away. The large areas either side of the chin can be cut away and the shoulders sloped back. The left shoulder is taken back more than the right because the head is turned slightly to one side. The back of the right shoulder is also brought forward slightly. The chin is undercut and the basic shape of the collar cut in. The extensions either side of the nose are removed and the hairline cut in. The waste on either side of the cheeks is also removed leaving the hairline at the sides. The eyebrows can be marked in and the wedge of the nose roughly shaped. All of this work is completed with a ½″ (12mm) No. 9 and ¾″ (19mm) No. 3. Accurate measurements must be made from the drawings using callipers.
4 The head above the hairline is roughly shaped into a dome, and the face is rounded back around the forehead, cheeks and jaw. Maintain the hairline. The eyes are hollowed out to the minimum depth and the mouth cut in to the level of the teeth. The clothes are given more shape and cut in around the neck. Accurate measurements from the drawings and constant reference to the photographs, or if possible the original, are vital. The chisels used are ½″ (12mm) No. 9, ⅜″ (9mm) No. 9, ¾″ (19mm) No. 3 and ½″ (12mm) No. 3.
5 The main lines of the hair are cut in with a V tool and the sides of the cut rounded off with a flat gouge, ½″ (12mm) No. 3. Further shaping and refining of the features is done with ½″ (12mm) No. 3, ¼″ (6mm) No. 3 and ⅜″ (9mm) No. 7. The teeth are roughly cut in and the bulbous eyeballs shaped. The upper and lower lids are drawn on this shape, and carefully cut in with a ⅜″ (9mm) No. 3. The eyeball is rounded smooth with a ¼″ (6mm) No. 2 and skew chisel. Further detail can be cut into the clothes.
6 All the features are refined and cleaned up

with rifler files and abrasive paper. Finally, the circle of the iris is carefully cut in with a gouge which perfectly fits the curvature. The pupil is cut in with a small No. 9. The hair and flesh are sanded smooth and the clothing left with a tooled finish.

Figure 1

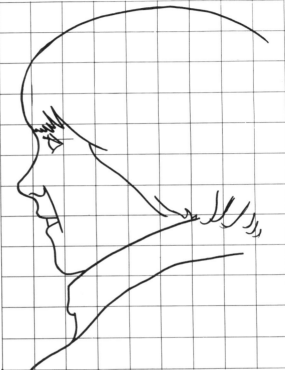

Figure 2

Figure 3

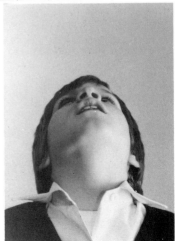

Figure 4

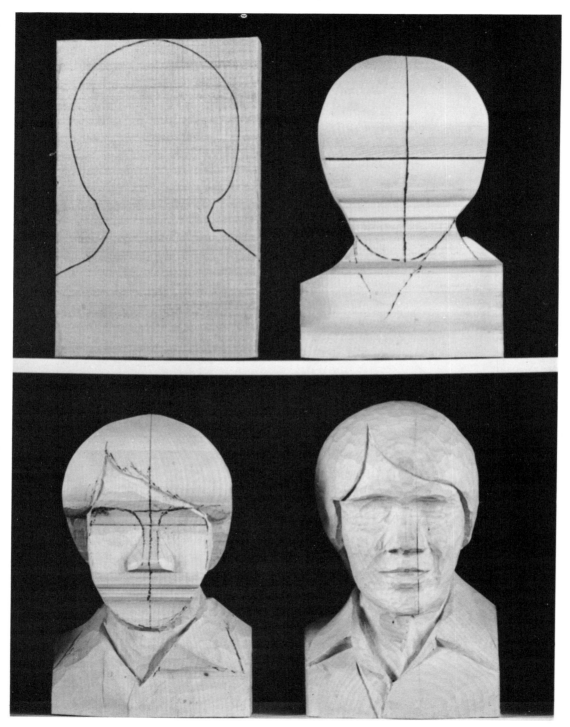

Figures 5–8

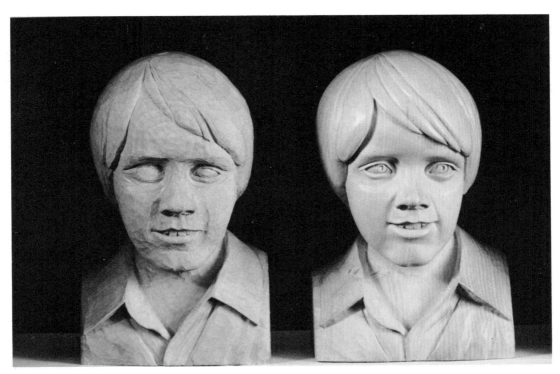

Figures 9 & 10

Introduction to Bird Carving

Birds are beautiful, fascinating and infinitely variable in their appearance and mannerisms. They are a popular subject for artists and sculptors in all media.

In wood, at least for the purist, they present a number of problems both technical and aesthetic. Most people identify birds mainly by their colouring. I have spoken to a wildlife photographer who, despite an encyclopaedic knowledge of birds could see no difference between different types of falcon without having some indication of the plumage colouration. Since colour is out of the question on an unpainted carving, the characteristic shapes and details of the bird must be accurately observed and carved. It might be wise to choose birds which are distinctive in some way other than colour. Another problem is the physical nature of feathers. Old carvings of birds frequently show the entire bird covered in clearly delineated feathers. They were carving the appearance of the bird, not the form. The majority of birds' plumage is more in the nature of fur than feathers and there is no tangible distinction or break between one feather and the next. Only colour renders the individual feathers visible. On a white dove or blackbird they are not nearly so clear. If you run your hand over a bird you will find that only the primaries and tail feathers can be distinguished separately, even on very large species. In my opinion, only these feathers need carving individually.

The legs present a serious technical problem. They are usually long and very thin, indeed looking at live specimens, it is remarkable just how slender they are. Some carvers solve this problem by using metal rods, even going so far as to shape the metal with files and so on, prior to painting them. If you see this as detracting from the integrity of wood sculpture to an unacceptable degree then the only answer is to support the weight of the bird in some other way. A glance at a book of bird photographs will show you that they frequently put themselves in positions where part of the body is in contact with the ground or branch. On a sloping perch only one leg will be extended, the other tucked under the breast which is pressing against the branch. On the ground, the tail or beak may touch the grass. Nevertheless, you will probably feel that the lightness of the creature can only be conveyed by showing it stood on its stilt-like legs, and if this is the case I suggest you make the body and legs separately, the latter being carved from wood selected to have the grain following the line of the bones. If the feathering around the thigh is then extended slightly downwards from the body and drilled to accept the leg, a reasonably strong construction will result. Let it be understood, it will be fragile, but so are those made by high-class porcelain companies and some study of these would be worthwhile.

BIRDS OF PREY

Birds of prey are unfailingly popular both with carvers and the general public. If you have seen the creatures sitting hunched on a post looking like a badly made hat you will realise that accuracy is not the most important point for consideration in the carving. This is really an exercise in aesthetic judgement – you must decide on the shape that you require, you must choose the features that you feel are significant and bring out the character of the falcon as you see it.

My own list of features is firstly the dead straight line from head to tip of the tail, tapering from the hunched shoulders to the point of the tail feathers. Secondly, the eyes must be finely carved, bulbous with the irises perfectly circular

1 Lugger Falcon

Figure 11

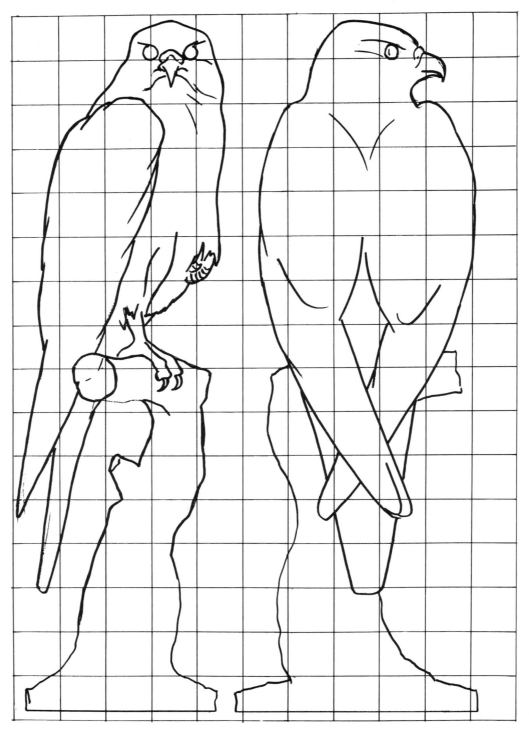

Figure 12

but the surrounding lids forming a tilted almond shape. The eyebrows must be tilted and scowling. Thirdly, the beak must be finely detailed and perfectly shaped into the needle-sharp hook. Finally, the feet must be sinewy and scaly, showing the knobbly joints and terminating in perfectly shaped talons.

Unless you do an immense amount of detail in the feathers, your falcon will finish as a fairly smooth uncomplicated carving, so the more detail you can put into the branch the better the contrast you will create. Go into the countryside and find an interesting piece of wood with flaking bark and a few broken twigs to use as a model, (see Kingfisher).

There is a technique which was used almost exclusively by carvers from Germany and Switzerland, frequently for the rendering of bark although it also succeeds very well for fur, stone and other textures. A little experimentation will be necessary to find the pattern you require, but

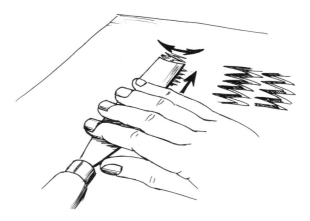

Figure 13

basically it involves holding a gouge hard against the wood at a low angle and rocking it from side to side as you push it forward, (Fig. 14). The shape of the gouge, forward movement, degree of rock and hand pressure will all vary the pattern.

Figure 14

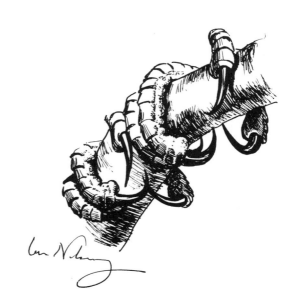

Figure 15 Lugger Falcon

2 Kingfisher

This beautiful bird which Tennyson described as "The secret splendour of the brooks", is rarely seen though not uncommon. The usual sighting is merely a brilliant flash of turquoise blue in the shadowy river bank.

Because of its dazzling colour I feel it needs a colourful piece of wood and for this reason I chose yew, the plan being that the white sapwood would appear in patches on the bird, contrasting with the orange heartwood. However, despite selecting the piece of timber carefully, it transpired that by the time the carving was finished not a shred of sapwood remained. Walnut would have been equally suitable.

The kingfisher has several unusual features: a very long beak and a short body that make him look badly proportioned; and feet that are small and weak and unlike those of most other birds (Fig. 18). The area around the eyes needs to be deeply cut and well defined to give the bird a touch of the preditor – he is, after all, a bird of prey.

One should contrive to make the branch a striking contrast to the sleek plumage of the bird. I think the only way to do this is to go out and find a suitably decayed or interesting piece of tree and copy it.

Although the carving is straightforward it is essential that the bird be completely finished before starting on the branch otherwise you may well find it virtually impossible to continue the bird on its fragile perch (Fig. 19).

Figure 16

Figure 17

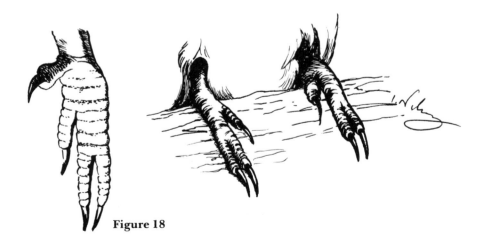

Figure 18

Figure 19

Figure 20

Figure 21

3   Peregrine Falcon

The vast majority of birds have legs so thin compared to the size of the body that a carving supported only by the legs would not survive unbroken. There are various ways of getting around this problem. The bird can be squashed down against its perch, as in the lugger falcon and the kingfisher, or it could be supported partly by the body touching a branch and one or both legs showing.

In this instance I have carved the bird with both legs completely free and a small branch touching the underside of the tail, thereby forming a tripod arrangement, which, whilst it is not strong, will give the carving enough strength to be handled and carefully moved around. This arrangement, although it gives a more active and lighter look to the bird, can appear somewhat contrived. It also creates problems in the carving process. Obviously the area between the tail, legs and branch cannot be sawn away with the rest of the profile. The body of the bird must be carved and finished as much as possible, leaving the support branch very strongly attached to the body. The main trunk of the branch can now be carved leaving only the legs and tail area to be completed.

The legs are roughly shaped out now, but still left strong, and the area under the tail reduced. The two parts must be worked together. If the legs were completed, any violent cut on the tail section might twist the bird enough to break the legs, and vice versa.

Finally only a portion of the supporting branch should be left to pare away, not touching the bird itself. Having done this, the carving must be complete. Even polishing must be done most carefully: a thin layer of sealer brushed on and sanded with the finest paper. Wax polish can be applied with a toothbrush.

The carving is mounted on a 6″ × 6″ × 3″ (152 × 152 × 76mm) block of blue Welsh slate to give it stability and prevent any casual movement by an observer.

Figure 22

Figure 23

Figure 24

Figure 26

Figure 25

Figure 27

4   Screech Owl

This is a somewhat different proposition to the peregrine falcon which has no serious structural difficulties because of the three point arrangement. The idea is that the owl is about to land on the branch and is supported only where its tail feathers touch a part of the tree. This means that this area must be left strong and intact for as long as possible.

The wings, which are relatively large, present the major technical difficulty. They require patience and precision to carve and great care not to break the feather tips. I found it beneficial to cut in the edges of the feathers with a scalpel which does not exert the same pressure as a chisel. The feet are not as delicate as the falcon's, but being smaller and feathered, need very precise carving to be convincing.

Figure 28

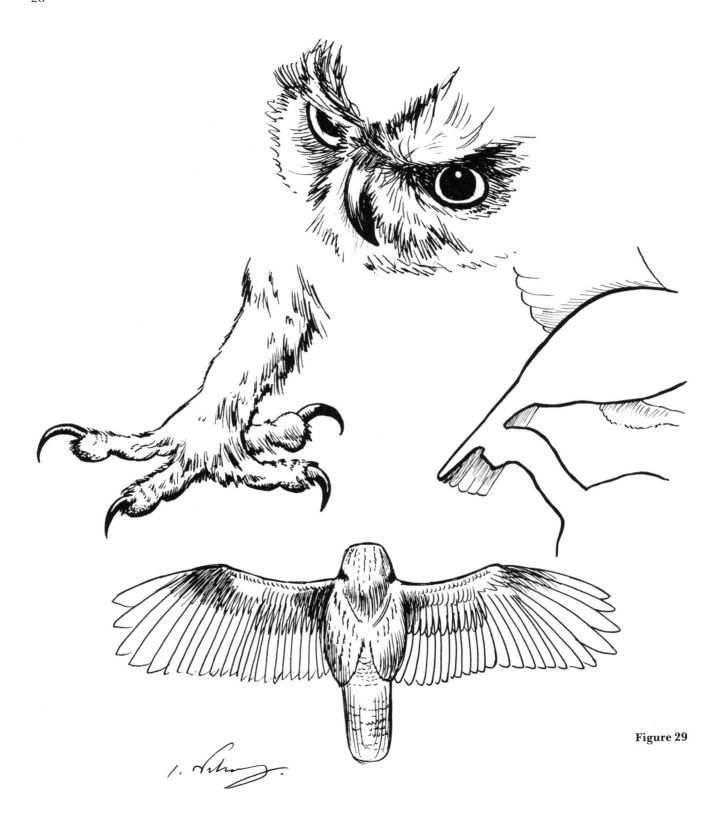

Figure 29

Figure 30

Figure 31

HORSES

5   Arab Stallion

There are, apparently, more horses now than at any time in history, also more hunting and racing. Horses can be seen in almost every environment from city police horses to the moorland pony. Their popularity as works of art in all media, and acceptability as ornaments in the home is almost unparalleled. They have always been a favoured subject for artists and sculptors and woodcarvers have been no exception.

Here we have an easily accessible live subject as well as a mass of photographic and sculptural reference material to enable the carver to gain a sound knowledge of the horse's conformation and anatomy. Certain aspects, however, tend to be overlooked by the observer and the photographer for obvious reasons: looking down on the top which is difficult, and looking from behind which is uninteresting and possibly dangerous. For this reason I have included studies of these views.

Assuming the carver knows what he has to carve, there are two major difficulties in carving a horse. The least problematic is the ears which, being thin, sharp and exposed, get broken both by carver and audience with amazing regularity; and once broken the piece is lost, particularly in the workshop where it inevitably falls on the floor amid a thousand similar chips of the same wood. I would therefore strongly recommend leaving the finishing of them till late in the carving and then binding them with adhesive tape. The other major problem is the legs – the design, carving and strength of them. It is fine to conceive a beautiful galloping stallion, but what has it got to stand on? Horses are rarely on more than two legs when moving and often only on one; and

many of the positions they adopt when running are ungainly and unbalanced. The carving of the legs is difficult in as much as its completion precludes further work on the body to a large extent. This means that the body and head must be virtually complete before the legs are hardly started. Fig. 33 shows the shaping-out stage ready for detailing, and the legs untouched. The body must then be held firmly in some way while the legs are carved, either upside down in the vice or flat on its side on the bench.

It is worth pursuing and perfecting the techniques, although they make for a disjointed sequence of work, because the ability to carve a horse can be applied to other animals as well. Once you understand how a horse works, a dog, cow, lion or elephant is not that different.

This horse is an Arab stallion, renowned for its beauty. Its chief features are a somewhat dished face, small ears, large eyes and nostrils, and a tail which, like the mane, is usually left long and is set higher on the rump, tending to be held up. Most noticeable though, is their lively, alert carriage and movement. This must be emphasised.

The horse is carved in limewood with an ebonised finish as described later in the rabbit project.

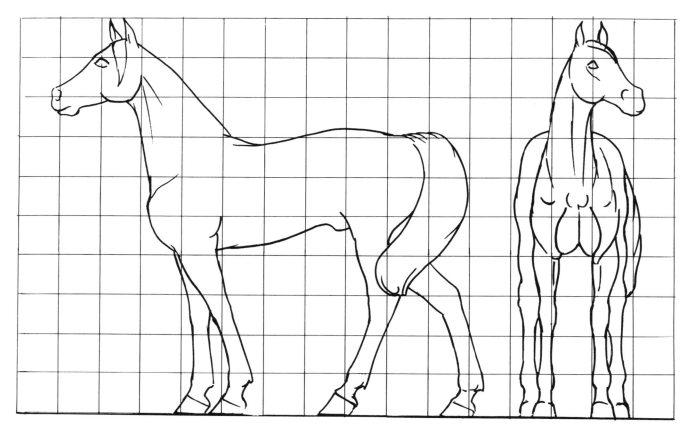

Figure 32

Figure 33

Figure 34

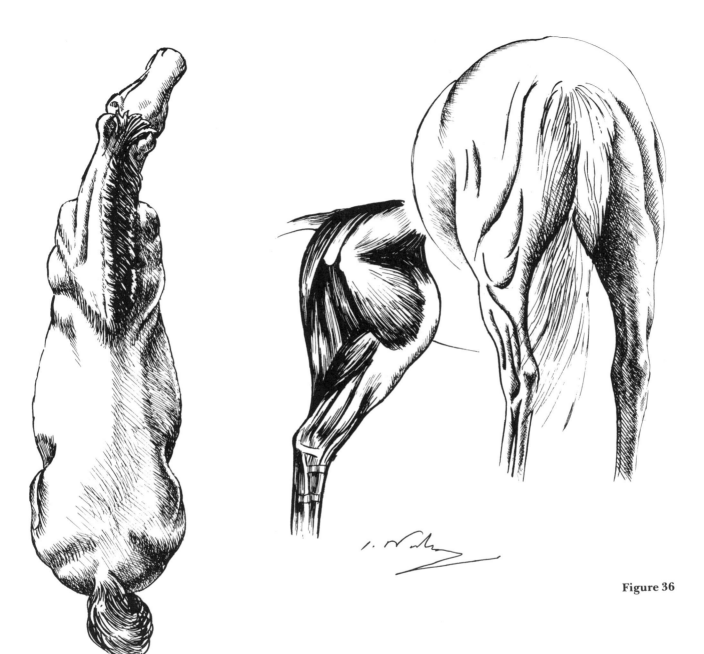

Figure 35

Figure 36

Figure 37

6 Head of a Racehorse

Figure 38

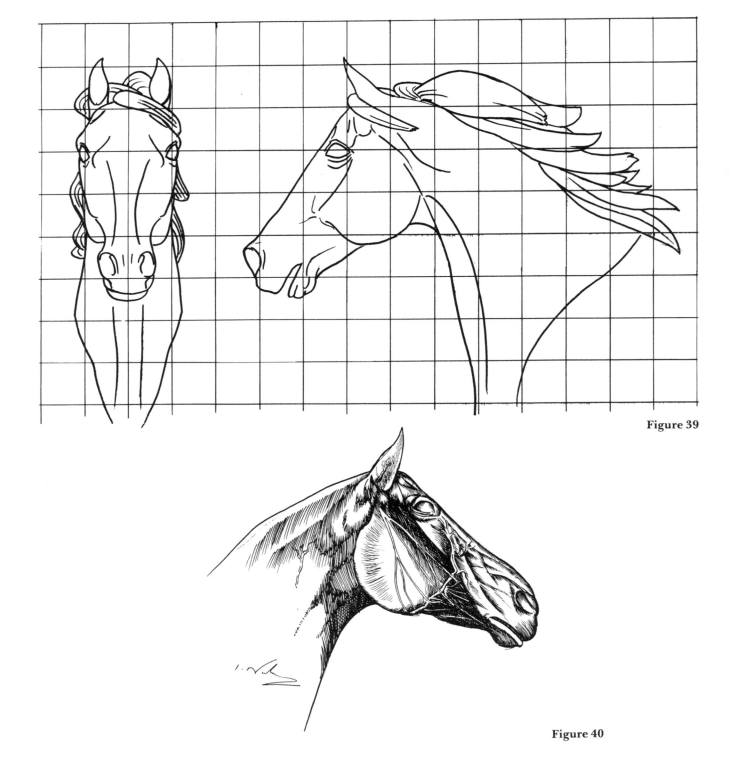

Figure 39

Figure 40

The difference between the superficial appearance of a low-bred rough-coated horse at rest in a field or loosebox, and a thoroughbred or Arab horse, finely groomed and in a state of high exertion and excitement is quite incredible. The eyes become wider and more prominent, the nostrils flare very widely, the mouth is probably open, and the veins, muscles and nerves stand out like ropes. Most of these features are more pronounced on the thoroughbred anyway.

As can be seen from my drawing, which might make a vet raise his eyebrows, the anatomical features of a horse's head are very complex, and these are only the main ones. On a real horse you will see the whole network of veins on the ears, neck, head, indeed the whole body. Were one to accurately carve all these, I think the result would be grotesque, but I think that a good effect can be achieved by careful tooling and sanding. For instance, the nerves which run down the cheek are not very prominent and form shallow ribs under the skin. If the depressions between these ribs are scooped out with a small gouge in one long clean cut, a sharp ridge will be left at the meeting point of the two cuts. If this ridge is then lightly sanded, it will just catch the light enough to give the appearance of a slight ripple in the surface. This same idea can be used on other areas of the head that are 'busy' with small muscles and veins. I find that a very satisfying surface can be achieved if the finished carving is carefully sanded with 300 grit silicon carbide paper using linseed oil as a lubricant – this gives a beautiful soft, smooth finish without removing any detail. Wipe off all the oil afterwards and leave it to dry for a couple of days. It can then be wax polished.

The flowing mane can be difficult depending on how elaborate you make it. The important thing is to establish the shapes of the main clumps of hair in some kind of rhythm and tool them to a smooth finish, see Fig. 41, establishing the smooth curves and undercuts. Then cut some lines into them, if you feel this is the effect you're aiming at. I used a ¼″ (6mm) No. 9 followed by a ⅛″ (3mm) No. 9 and 1/16th″ (1.5mm) No. 12 (Fig. 42).

The most difficult thing is to judge when you have done enough.

Figure 41

Figure 42

Figure 43

7 Shire Horse

Shires really are massive; huge, solid bones in thick bulging muscles. I think that once having seen heavy horses in the flesh the prospect of reducing one to a few inches high seems rather preposterous. However, the carts that they pull are frequently reduced in that way and no doubt many model makers have wished they had carved a horse to complement their dray or carriage.

I set out to carve the shire in the same way as any other horse but when I had reached the stage when the whole horse was fairly smoothly tooled I felt that the feel of the animal was already achieved and that further detail would not improve it.

It is always a good thing to sit back and look at what you are carving and ask yourself whether the features you are including are really contributing anything to the sculpture as a whole. Sometimes, seemingly important details must be sacrificed to the overall effect. Some people might find this shire horse lacking in the detail of the feathering on the feet and the mane, both typical features of the breed, but I think that to anyone familiar with them, these things are suggested sufficiently strongly for them to be seen in the mind, in the same way that one would recognise a word with a letter missing.

The horse is carved from a very beautiful piece of walnut, highly sanded and polished and mounted on burr oak.

Figure 44

Figure 45

Figure 46

Figure 47

Figure 48

8   Finishing Line

This carving was conceived as a single racehorse, the second one being added at the request of the purchaser.

The first stage in the process was to employ a professional photographer who could take reasonable pictures at distance, using a mechanical film winder enabling the camera to record the movement of the horse five times per second. One position was selected and the picture used as the basis for the carving. This was then copied exactly in the form of a model or *maquette* about 5″ (125 mm) high (See Fig. 51). It will be seen that the figure on the left is exactly the same as the photograph – the jockey looking ahead. Two faults were found with this design: the rider seemed somewhat uninteresting, and the whole piece was very front heavy. I therefore decided to turn the jockey's head and bring back his whip

hand, and to move the single support leg further forward to equalise the balance. This is the model on the right, which was then carved on the final larger scale from a solid block of walnut.

The whole carving has a tooled finish, but I have attempted to use the toolcut to express minor details such as the heavily veined area on the back leg (See Fig. 54). This can be more successful than finely carved veins which may look very overworked. I think it also gives the piece more movement.

Similarly, the eyeball is slightly faceted to catch the light, (see Fig. 55) and the jockey's eyes are drilled to give them directional appearance (see Fig. 53). The reins are made from shavings of walnut, cut into strips, and soaked in boiling water to make them supple and glued into place. The rings in the bit are turned boxwood. The

Figure 49

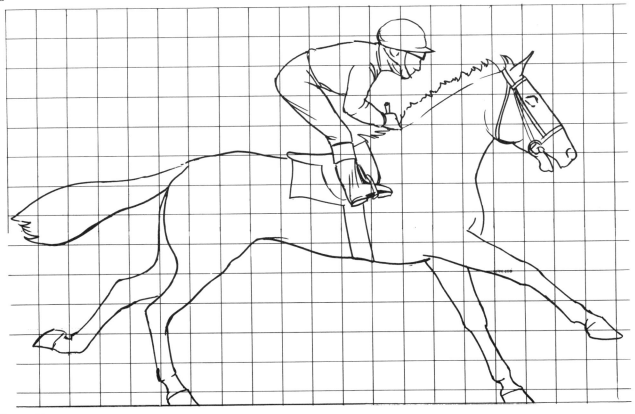

Figure 50

bridle and bit are drilled, the ring split on one side and fed through these holes and re-glued (also seen in Figs 52 and 55).

The white sapwood on the horse's nose was fortuitous, but looked so much as if it were stuck on that I darkened it somewhat with stained oil. The whip was made separately and inserted in the hole drilled in the hand.

The wood had been selected so that the grain ran up the supporting leg and this was drilled and screwed to the base. The finish is a light coat of linseed oil.

Although the carving wobbles slightly when moved, there has been so sign of the leg being under undue stress. However, the problems of carving a horse are obvious and have been discussed earlier. It is sufficient to say that particular attention at the outset – right at the planning stage – must be given to the problems of stability and balance and to structural strengths and weaknesses.

Figure 51

Figure 52

Figure 53

Figure 54

Figure 55

Figure 56

9 Polo

Figure 57

Polo is said to be one of the fastest sports; certainly the sight of a group of mounted men charging around a field at full gallop and whirling long mallets around looks to the layman like a very expensive way of killing yourself. The relatively few rules are designed for safety, but horses and men have scars to prove that rules are made to be broken.

The horses are specially bred and trained to be completely controllable by one hand. The mane is invariably shaved and the tail bound up with tape, or plaited. I think what strikes one immediately about polo ponies (more accurately, polo horses) is the leather straps and ropes that festoon them. There are five or seven reins leading from the head, depending on the type of bit used. They are used to control lateral and vertical movement of the head, speed and braking. They also have two chest bands, one over the shoulders, and a belly band, and of course a heavy saddle and stirrups. In addition the legs are bound with thick cloth and tape or leather gaiters. The rider has a helmet, strapped under the chin; gloves, knee-pads and spurred boots. He carries the mallet and a whip, completing the picture of a travelling saddlery (Fig. 58).

An expert player explained the rules of the game to me and I learnt many facts vital to the accuracy of the carving. For instance, contrary to my belief, the ball is hit with the side of the mallet, not the end. Also the horses must not touch in front of the saddle, i.e. shoulder to shoulder. This point was most important because I planned for the two horses to be pinned together. Galloping horses rarely have more than one foot on the ground, and having one horse on two feet and the other on one, I could create a tripod effect and the two then locked together with a steel dowel (Fig. 61). The situation in the original drawing, taken from a photograph, is in fact, a foul. My advisor told me that a carving of a foul-situation would be of no interest to polo players. This is a good example of the folly of using photographs without knowledge!

Each horse and rider is made from a solid block of walnut. Certain accessories however are separate. The mallets are made in two parts and inserted into a hole drilled in the hand. The whip is similarly made and fitted. The rings of the bit are made from boxwood, with a tiny dowel to insert into the mouth. The straps that are tight to the body are carved, i.e. the belly strap, the chest bands and the bridle. The reins are made from veneer-thin strips of walnut, including the thin running rein that passes through the bit ring. Using information supplied by my adviser I used a system of reins that was less complicated.

Research is essential for a carving of this complexity. I certainly used six or seven books on horses, a pile of polo magazines and many hours spent 'studying the horses and talking to the players. All these sources are easily enough obtained and players are only too keen to show you the ropes.

The finish is finely tooled and given a light coat of linseed oil – turpentine mixture. Once finished it can never really be polished again because of the fine detail of the tack. The horses are mounted on green Westmoreland slate, the hooves having been drilled and screwed up through the stone (Fig. 60).

Figure 58

Figure 59

Figure 60

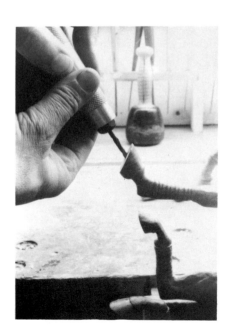

Figure 61 The feet are screwed to the base at A, B, and C, and the
bodies joined by a steel dowel at D.

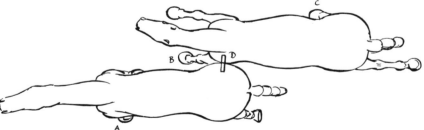

Figure 62

STUDIES FROM NATURE

10 Adder

These are very easy carvings to do and can be most effective. Snakes seem incapable of adopting a position that is not beautiful, interesting, elegant or dramatic. I see no point in trying to reproduce the thousands of scales that cover the surface. We are dealing not with an object of study, but a sensual experience for the hand and eye, whether you see snakes as beautiful if dangerous creatures, or disgusting reptiles.

My snakes were inspired by the adder, families of which, apparently, infest a local beauty spot. I felt that their simple shape deserved an exotic wood and Mexican rosewood is one that is still a reasonable price and readily available, and is particularly vivid in colour. It is rather hard but not like blackwood or ebony.

The main outline is bandsawn. The pierced sections are taken out with a coping saw or drilled out. Then screw the snake upside down to a piece of waste board, carefully placing the screws in areas which will be cut away when the

Figure 63

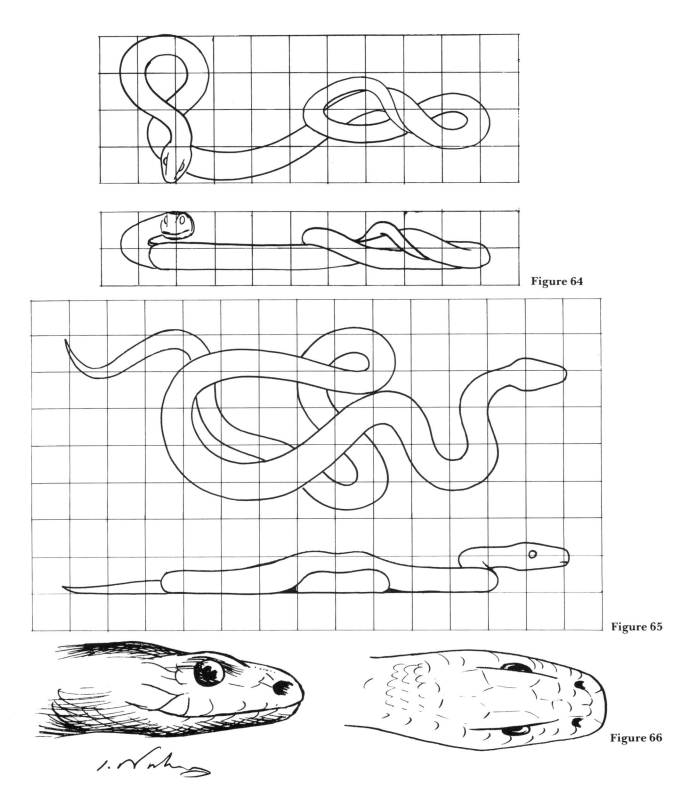

Figure 64

Figure 65

Figure 66

upper section is carved. Having fixed it down firmly, carve the underside of the snake, allowing a slight squashing of the overlapping parts of the body. The head is slightly raised, as though preparing to strike, but that is a personal decision. Having finished the underside as far as possible turn the snake over and screw it to the wasteboard from underneath, topside up. You can now finish the carving having already completed the undercutting.

When I had reached a fairly advanced well-tooled stage, I filed the snake smooth, followed by thorough sanding to the finest degree. The eyes were then drilled out and turned pegs of ebony with rounded tops were glued into place. The whole was finally waxed. (No sealer is really necessary on rosewood).

I felt that stone was the ideal surface to mount the snake on and settled for the fairly plain, green Westmoreland slate. I feel that a wooden plinth would really kill the whole thing.

All in all, this was an expensive carving in terms of wood and stone, but cheap on labour and most impressive.

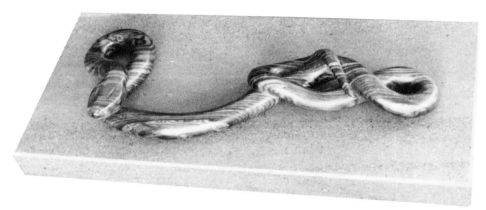

Figure 67

Figure 68

11   Snails

Spirals occur in nature in many forms. There are two basic types: the equable or Archimedean, and the equiangular or logarithimic. In the Archimedean spiral, the distance between each succeeding spiral is always the same, as in the case of a coiled rope. What concerns us in this project is the equiangular spiral in which the whorls continously increase in breadth and do so in a steady and unchanging ratio. These spirals manifest themselves in shells, flowers, fir cones, horns and numerous other ways. Rather than draw this subject, I have shown photographic examples of the snail in four studies (a, b, c and d) and two further examples of more advanced shell forms toward which you might progress.

The squared-up drawings show the spirals as having quite definite measurable proportions and these can be used to help when planning, or roughing out, your carving. Thus in the drawing ab is ⅓ of bc, de is ⅓ of ef and gh is ⅓ of hi, and so on in any and every position. This is the ratio for the nautilus shell. The amazing variety and beauty this simple principle creates is quite staggering; shells of amazing complexity and subtlety can be found.

Leckhampton Hill in the Cotswolds abounds with huge Roman snails. Their shells are delightful objects to handle and the fascination of the spiral combined with the large smooth curves seem to be asking you to carve it, especially if you have a showy piece of wood that might be useless for anything more complex.

I used the end of a log of yew, somewhat shaken and faulty, but with wild swirling grain and a lovely colour. The carving is fairly simple, unless you try to hollow out the shell, in which case it will become very difficult.

Yew wood achieves a superb finish, but it requires sanding to a very high degree. Its hard, fine texture will show scratches from the finest grit. I spent a lot of time with fine steel wool and wax, and finally a motorised buffing wheel, but its final finish will be the result of months of daily polishing.

(a)

(b)

(c)

(d)

Figure 69

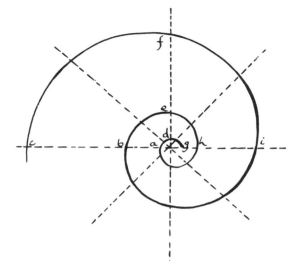

Figure 70

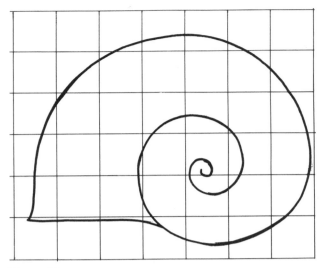

Figure 71

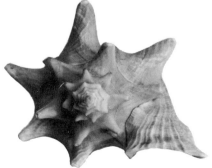

Figure 72

Figure 73

12   Frog

Here is a subject that seems to be very popular these days. Many gift shops are stocked with frogs of every size, shape and colour in plastic, metal, china, resin and other materials that can be shaped.

Most of them are very unlifelike, mainly because, I think, people don't really want a slimy, wet-looking frog with every spot and wart on it sitting on their sideboard. I suggest that your design should be as simplified or as stylised as you wish.

They are simple shapes to carve and do not take up too much wood. The toes are thin and wiggly, seeming to have no bones, and the legs bend all over the place. I suppose the most prominent feature is the eyes which need to be carved very bulbously, perhaps even exaggerated.

If the frog is to be mounted on a flat base like mine, it is best to carve the underside at an early stage while it can be held upside down in the vice without danger.

Mine was carved from teak and on reflection I think that a prettier wood would have made more of the carving, perhaps rosewood or yew.

Figure 74

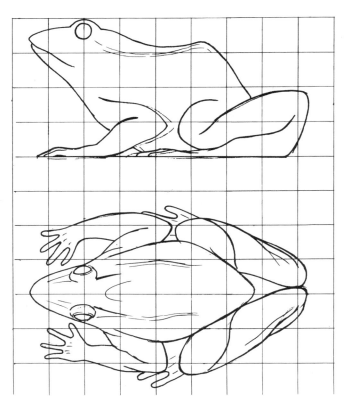

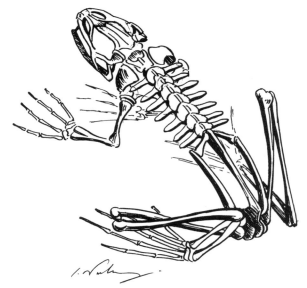

Figure 76

Figure 75

Figure 77

13 Trout

Figure 78

For this carving I used a log of mulberry about 4″ (100mm) thick, which had a lot of small burrs in the surface. It was about one year cut, and really ought to have cracked, but didn't. I find that carved green wood rarely cracks if it is treated reasonably, though it is not a practice I would recommend.

For this carving buy a trout from your fishmonger or fish farm. An excellent 'live' model can be purchased at a very moderate cost.

I propped up my model into a curve with pieces of stick on a plate and froze it solid into the shape I had decided upon. Once hard, I could impale it on a spike to maintain the shape and work at my own pace. The fish could be replaced in the freezer as and when necessary during the progress of the work.

Mulberry cuts very easily and cleanly and the shape of the fish is quite simple. The fins need a little care, but that is after you have carved them, in the sanding and polishing. If you wish, you can mark in the scales on the body surface, although I personally see no point in it; there is no dimension in them so it would be as a decorative appearance only. The water is an attempt to give movement, and throw the fish up. Large smooth cuts are needed in curves echoing the shape of the fish.

A word of warning when using green wood: dampness or water will come out of the base onto the surface the carving is stood on, so take extra care if this is displayed on a piece of furniture.

Figure 79

Figure 80

14   Polecat

Figure 81

Oriental wood and ivory carvings frequently have features inlaid with bone ivory, horn etc. Whilst this is occasionally seen in European carving it is not common and I felt this technique would be ideal on the polecat because the gleaming black eyes set in the dark fur and the vicious teeth seem to be such a feature of the animal. Once common, this most destructive of creatures is now relatively rare. Stuffed examples, of course, can be seen in museums, and the ferret is a domestic hybrid of the white Asiatic polecat.

The timber used, wenge, appears a dark, rich brown, but is made up of fine black and orange stripes. It is hard, splintery and difficult to work but polishes up beautifully. The pores are so large that they leave noticeable holes in the surface.

The eye sockets were first carved into oval hollows, then drilled to accept the ebony eyes. These were carved and filed, not turned, so that the eye was slightly oval, with a small dowel on the back. The ebony was given several coats of

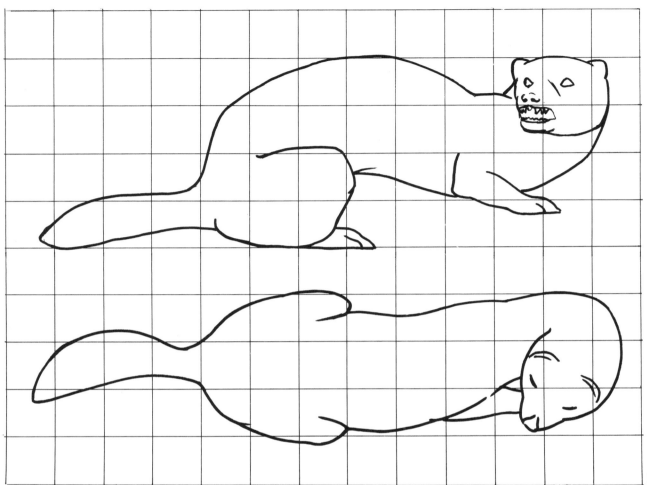

Figure 82

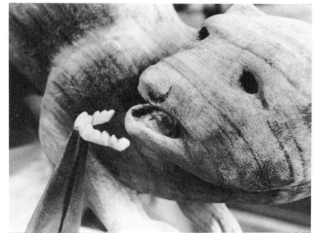

Figure 83

Figure 84

french polish to give it a brilliant shine.

The teeth were made from a small piece of ivory, but bone would be just as good. Select a piece of bone in which the curve of the cylinder approximates that of the jaws. Pare this down to about 2mm. thick. You will find that bone and ivory work in a similar way to wood. The shape of the teeth can now be made with a three cornered file. Sand with the finest abrasive paper and burnish with metal polish. The set of teeth is cut off with a fret saw and the jaw then carefully incised with a small gouge to form a groove to fit the teeth which are glued in place. Repeat this for the other jaw (Fig. 83).

The polecat is mounted on a slab of quartz, but any stone or contrasting piece of wood will suffice.

Figure 85

15 The Tamworth Pig

Figure 86

This Tamworth pig may look rather like any other pig to the layman and I think most of the difference is in the colour, and the shape of the body – that is the size and the number of pork chops that can be made from it. I saw this ancient breed of pig at the rare breeds survival centre in the Cotswolds. My first inclination was to produce a family group, but I decided on this more formal portrait.

I soon realised that I would never persuade a pig to sit and scratch itself while I studied its shape, so I adapted a rather overweight labrador. The balance of the body and the way the weight is thrown on to one buttock is the crucial factor to look for. It may soon become apparent to you, that your knowledge of pigs has been conditioned by cartoon characters and that further investigation is necessary. A trip to the

Figure

Figure 88   **Figure 89**   **Figure 90**

butcher and a moderate outlay will secure you a pig's head and trotters. This will provide a perfect model for the only real detail on the animal. It is amazing how much like the cartoons pigs really are, and they appear to smile happily even in death. The ears are truly huge and the feet tiny and pointed, and the joints in the legs are more subtle than in many animals. The tail is quite delicate, but I feel it really must be quite long and curly.

Sycamore is a pleasant wood to carve and takes an excellent finish. However, you will find that very thorough sanding is necessary to achieve the smooth porky look of the soft but heavy muscles. The holes in the nose I did with a dental burr and the eyes are recessed using a small No. 9 gouge.

Figure 91

Figure 92

16   Lop Eared Rabbit

This ancient breed of domestic rabbit lends itself to a simple sculpture executed as an experiment in finishing rather than carving. The animal's body is so soft and mobile that only the bare essentials of its bodily outline need be adhered to and few tools are needed to complete it. My carving is slightly smaller than a full grown buck, and I confess I have never seen a totally black one.

The carving finished, the piece becomes an exercise in sanding and painting. The sanding need not go to the level of fineness required for a normal wax polished finish, but after rubbing down with 120 grit, stain the whole carving black. I used spirit stain with about 25% shellac sealer added. Rub down with very fine paper and repeat the process of staining. The carving should now be completely black and very smooth although, no doubt, some surface blemish will have appeared. Now paint the carving with matt black paint, the type used for painting wrought iron is fine. Use a large, soft sable-type brush. Repeat five or six times until a thick dense layer of paint has been built up. Now, using the finest abrasive paper rub down the paint. This is best done when the paint has had three or four days to harden. It must be done very carefully and meticulously to achieve a flawless, smooth surface, obliterating all brush marks, but not going through to the wood on the corners. Nevertheless, the worst will probably happen and white patches appear. These can be touched up with

Figure 93

the earlier mixture of black stain and sealer.

Now add 25% of french polish to the black stain creating a thin black polish. Using the paint brush, paint the rabbit quickly with the black polish being careful to avoid edges drying and creating lines in the finish. Those skilled with french polishing techniques may prefer to use a rubber, but I am not. Others may like black lacquer, but I think french polish is best. Repeat this exercise until you are satisfied that the rabbit has an immaculate, highly gloss, black surface. After a day or two to dry, polish with black wax.

Figure 94

Figure 95

17   Hereford Bull

When I first investigated bulls with a view to carving one, I found out a few facts which rather surprised me. My idea of a bull was a large animal with huge powerful shoulders, a thick muscular neck, large horns and a drooping fold of skin hanging down its chest. The sort of thing that is seen in bullrings. I went to a farm where Hereford bulls are bred and was pleasantly surprised by the enthusiastic reception I received.

This is quite common, I find; people who are proud of their great interest in life are only too pleased to help anyone who wants to know about it.

The prize bull was hosed down, brushed and held by the nose while I photographed him.

What surprised me was that he wasn't just big, he was huge, but completely docile. The stockman explained that horns had been done away

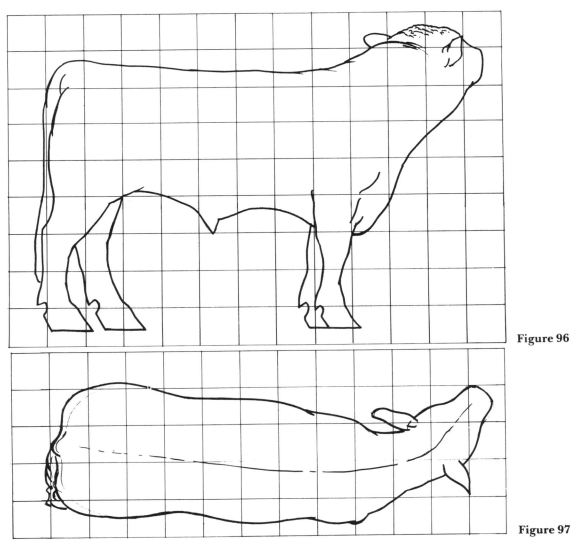

Figure 96

Figure 97

with years ago. The huge shoulders and small hips were poison to him. The best meat is on the back end, so good bulls have big beam ends, and the loose skin at the front is not a very good feature. The head in relation to the bulk seems small and the legs short and thick. The coat is rough, the fur seeming to go in all directions and is very tightly curled on the forehead. Most important, there is virtually no sign of muscles – the limbs are flat and shapeless as if the whole animal were padded with inches of fat.

My butcher said his idea of a Hereford bull was "all straight lines". This is certainly true of the back and hind quarters which form a perfect right angle with a sharp corner at the root of the tail.

I used brown oak for its colour and robustness and portrayed the bull bellowing, which it did incessantly.

I felt the only treatment which would suit this monster was to use a pattern of large facets to form the planes of the body. So I used the largest, flattest gouge I had, a 1¼″ (31mm) No. 2, and cut the main shapes of the head, neck, body and hind quarters with the greatest economy I could, using small tools only on the legs and details. The curls on the head I did by toolcuts with a ¼″ (6mm) No. 12 in all directions. Only the muzzle was sanded. The carving was oiled and wax polished.

Figure 98

18 St. George's Mushrooms

Figure 99

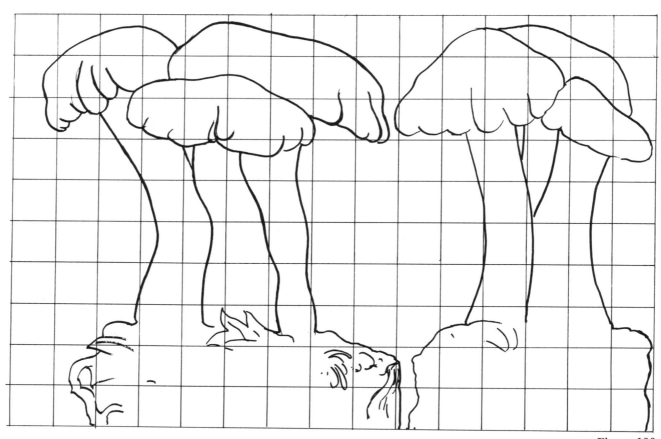

Figure 100

Figure 101

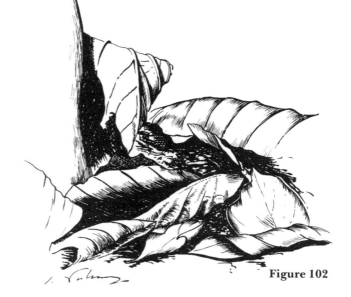

Figure 102

Walking across a bare hillside in the early autumn, I saw a clump of large white mushrooms standing alone in the grass like a Stone Age relic. For most people fungus of any type seems to fascinate and repel at one and the same time, somehow inciting them to make a closer inspection, and then usually to kick the thing to pieces.

My first idea was to carve the mushrooms in a light wood and place a creature of some kind on top, a toad or dragonfly, in a darker wood. But I decided to make the plants themselves the main objects and the ground below them the detail. I used an old oak beam, dark brown in colour and apparently cut from a pollarded or burry tree.

Carving the mushrooms is fairly straightforward, the piercing between the stalks is tedious, but not difficult. The collection of leaves, nuts, roots and soil that makes up the base, was done in a purely arbitrary fashion, simply using features as I fancied. Use was made of splitting the wood and scrubbing out the grain with a wire brush to reveal the curly knots and fibres. Much of the piercing and undercutting of the roots was completed with rotary burrs in a flexible shaft and punches were also used to create a variety of textures. Most of the carving was sanded although some was left tooled and the cracks in the beam filled with black resin.

This is a highly pleasing carving both to hand and eye, which, requiring no great accuracy, can be designed to suit the ability and ambition of the carver.

Figure 103

THE HUMAN FORM

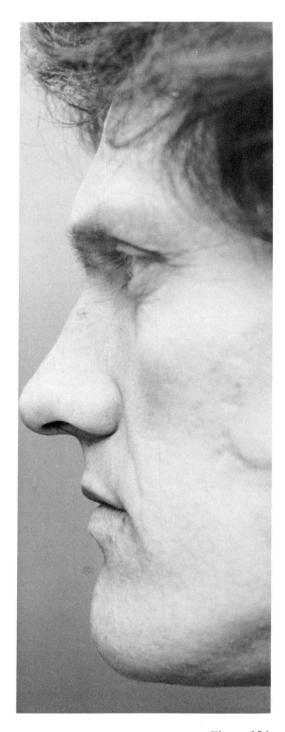

Figure 104

19   Self-Portrait

Virtually all artists have done a self-portrait at least once, and some many times, no doubt for a variety of reasons. My own reason was that I thought it would be ideal from the modelling point of view – nobody is likely to sit for the length of time it takes to do a wood carving, and I think it is only by having a real head to work from, every inch of the way, that one can really learn what a head is like. It is a very interesting exercise and an extremely valuable one.

It requires a large block to get anything near lifesize. Mine is ¾ actual size and the back of the head is cut off flat where the bark of the tree started. A fairly plain wood is best, such as lime, sycamore or a straight grained piece of oak. The cherry that I have used is rather strongly figured and this tends to create distractions and optical illusions on the features.

I used a photograph for the profile which was bandsawn and a mirror for the front view which is not really worth bandsawing. The trouble with using a mirror is that the image is reverse, and this will come across in the carving. The other problem is that every time you look in the mirror you have the look of concentration which is difficult to rid yourself of, and this also will come out in the carving.

I was not terribly bothered about achieving a perfect likeness, but since you can look at, and feel and measure every feature you should achieve a reasonable similarity to your face.

The eyes are always a problem. Do you leave them as blank eyeballs, do you mark in the iris as I have done, or do you cut a hole for the pupil? It is really a matter of personal choice. Look at some sculptures of heads and see the different effects; see also *Alexander the Great* project.

I tooled the hair quite roughly and sanded the flesh very smooth, which is what I usually do on a head, but I can envisage a more rugged or older face that might well look better tooled.

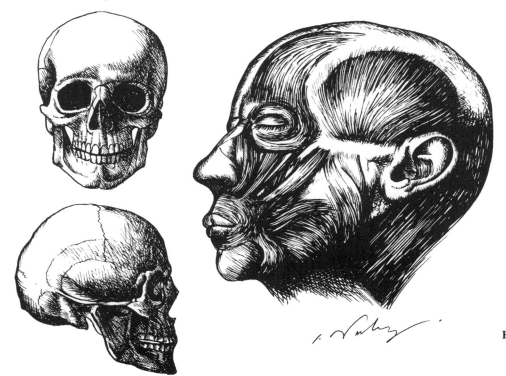

Figure 105

Figure 106

20 Portrait of Alexander

Figures 107 & 108

An undertaking to carve someone's portrait should not be taken lightly. Their idea of what they look like and what you see may be somewhat different. Add to that the errors of drawing and carving and the obvious difference between wood and flesh and the possibilities of disagreement with your sitter are quite apparent. When the total figure is only nine inches (229mm) high the chances of achieving a good likeness are lessened yet again. Also in the case of young people the facial features are less defined and more difficult to delineate. The approach to a carving such as that of Alexander must, then, be tackled from a different attitude to that of, say, a figure of a workman or dancer for example, who has a mature face with distinctive features and whose likeness is not required to please anyone in particular.

It is demonstrably true that recognition of a person springs primarily from the general shape of the head and body, the posture and the way their clothes hang on them. This, then, is your first line of attack. You must see the person and study them at home in their normal routine so that you can become familiar with the shape and mannerisms. Copious photographs are needed, in Alexander's case, 72, and if possible, typical poses taken by a close friend or relative of the subject. Close-ups of details – hands, feet and head, are essential and good profiles and front and rear views of the head must be obtained.

The prime target of the drawings, then, will be to obtain very accurate and recognisable outlines of the subject. If these are then transferred to the block, and equally accurately bandsawn, you will have succeeded in crossing a major hurdle in obtaining a likeness in the carving.

Proceed in the normal way, retaining as much as possible the outline you have cut. As the carving progresses study the profiles on other photographs taken from different angles and try to incorporate these in the carving. If this is successful, fine details such as eyes, lips, etc. will merely add to the likeness rather than create it.

Boxwood is undoubtedly the wood for work of this kind, though fruitwood, such as pear, or a very fine timber such as hawthorn, might suffice.

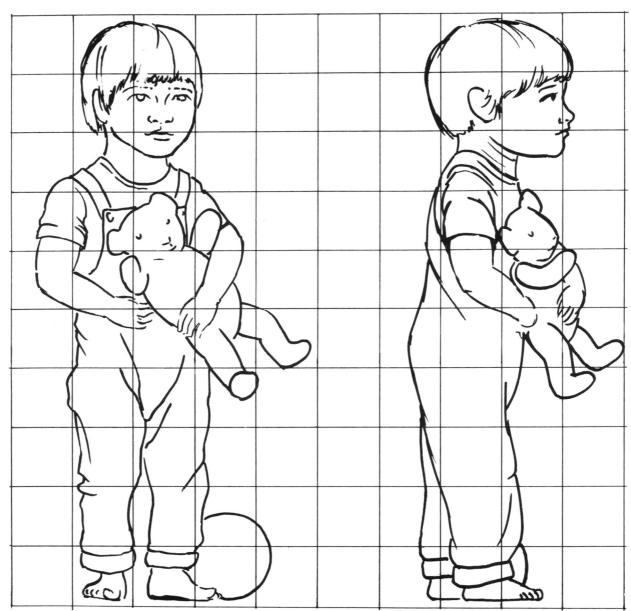

Figure 10

Figure 110

21   Reclining Nude

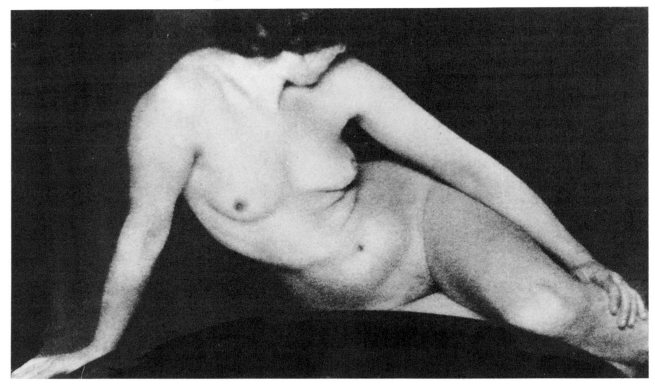

Figure

The nude human figure has inspired such enormous quantities of works of art for so many hundreds of years that it raises the question – what is the fascination? Whether there is some deep seated psychological motive for the desire to reproduce flesh and blood in stone, wood, metal, paint etc., I am not in a position to judge, but the fact is that the impulse exists among virtually all artists when faced with a live model.

This nude was not in fact inspired by a live model but by a small old print I noticed in a photographer's studio.

Having seized the picture, it was enlarged and carried off to my workshop. It is rather grainy but perfectly good enough to work from. I then seized a young lady and prevailed upon her to model for me.

Using the largest piece of limewood I had available, I still finished up with a fairly small carving. The human form is very subtle and the slight undulations of the surface on this reduced scale are almost non-existent. What may seem to be a very slight scoop of the gouge in the rough, will appear as a hard deep cavity when polished. Photography emphasises this effect, and although the actual carving looks better than my photograph of it, nevertheless I feel that my nude is perhaps less feminine than I would have liked.

The main technical difficulties are in holding. There is only a narrow line along the buttock, thigh and calf that can be screwed into and this must be accurately located in order to fix the piece to a block for holding in the vice. The free standing arm is obviously vulnerable to breakage and cannot really be screwed. I therefore held the palm to the block with double sided adhesive tape. The other difficulty is sanding which must be exceptionally thorough and careful to achieve the softness of a woman's body.

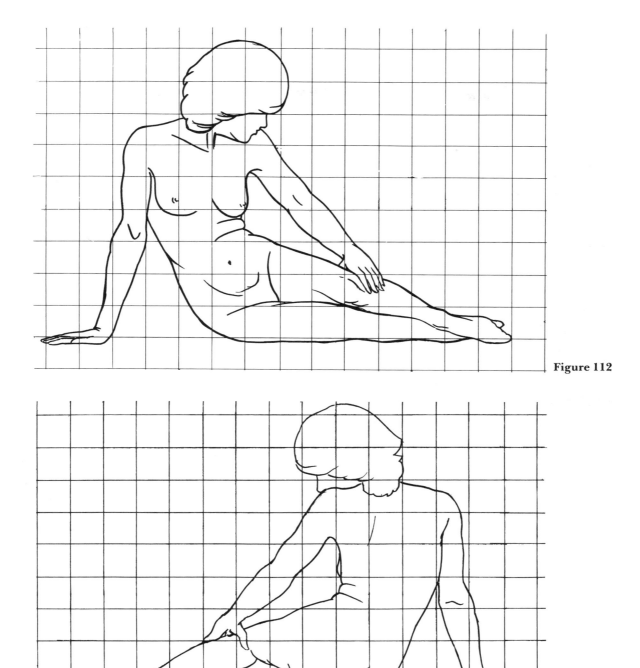

Figure 112

Figure 113

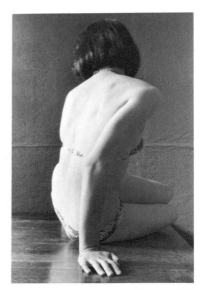

Figure 114

Figure 115

Figure 116

Figure 117

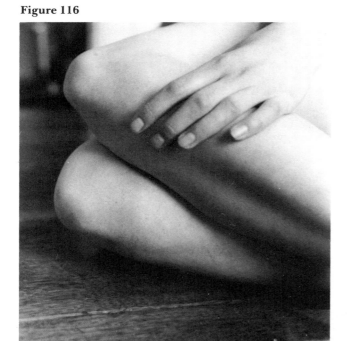

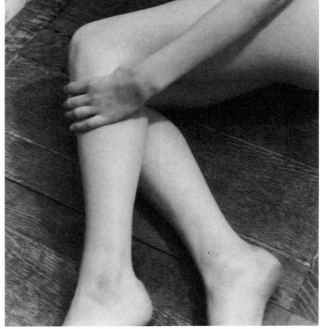

Figure 118

Figure 119

22 Standing Nude

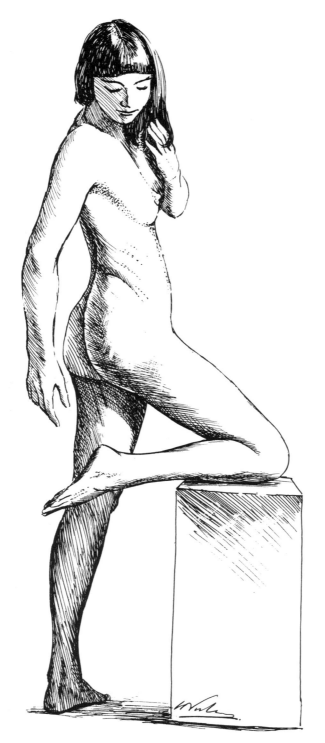

Figure 120

This carving came about as a consequence of a particular piece of wood, a log of apple, which I bought from the family of a deceased cabinet maker. I had no great expectation of it, seeing the usual shakes in the end, but after trimming it down from both ends I found that the cracks extended only a few inches. After squaring the 14″ (355mm) diameter log, I ended up with a 9″ (229mm) square block, 23″ (585mm) long, of bone dry, virtually flawless apple wood. Now that is a very rare commodity and I thought long and hard about what to use it for.

Eventually, I resolved upon a nude which would show off this lovely wood and provide an excellent subject for the beautiful finish and feel for it, and, into the bargain, it would be most enjoyable carving it.

The original pose was inspired by a drawing in an anatomy book which I then had my model imitate while I took my photographs. The only way to reproduce a human figure accurately is with a live model posing throughout the work, but failing this, photographs are second best. However, I find that when I carve a nude I am automatically inclined to alter the forms to those shapes I think are more pleasant. It is not often one has the chance to play God.

The main problem with the carving, apart from knowing the subject, is the strength of the legs when they are thinned down and for this reason I finished the body completely before doing the legs. Incidentally, whilst I carved the block on which she is kneeling, in situ, in the solid, I wanted it dead square and smooth so I cut it off, planed it and dowelled it back on. The other problem was the prodigious amount of sanding necessary to achieve the silk-smooth finish that can be had from apple wood.

Figures 121–123

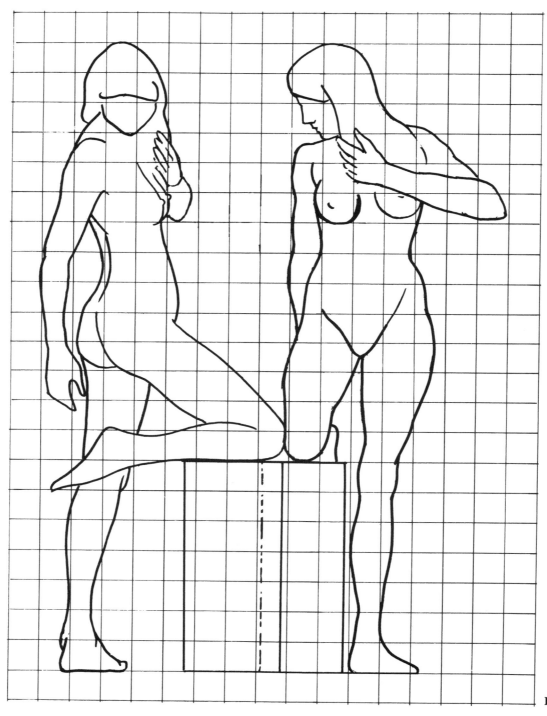

Figure 124

Figure 125

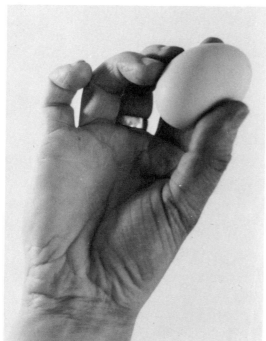

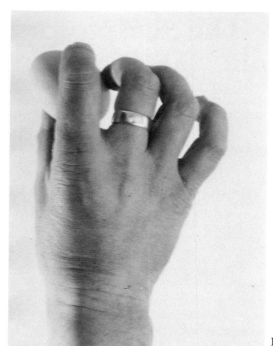

Figure 126

Figure 128

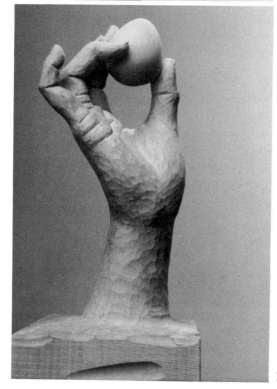

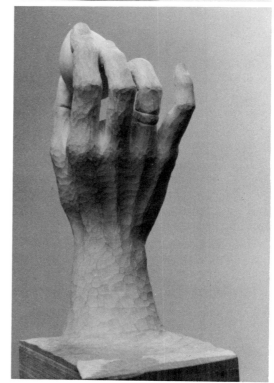

Figure 127

Figure 129

23   The Sculptor's Hand

Hands are always said to be very difficult to portray in painting or sculpture. This is certainly true in so far as our critical faculty is greatly enhanced by our intimate knowledge of their structure. As with a portrait, we are immediately aware of any deviation from the normal hand, even allowing for the peculiarities of the individual. However, the fact that they present us with a perfect model and source of reference makes them a highly recommended subject for carving.

I chose to have my hand holding an egg primarily because I wanted it in a position of tension, but with the fingers open. An egg in particular was chosen because I felt it would give a certain symbolism, 'the strong hand holding the delicate egg of a future generation'. And finally the fact that adduction – the ability to hold an object between thumb and finger – is said to be the principal distinguishing physical ability that makes man unique among the animals.

The work of the French sculptor Rodin is worth studying. He carved a number of hands in marble, notably *Cathedral*, a pair of hands held vertically, and *The Hand of God*, a single hand holding a rock from which a male and female nude are emerging. Looking at these sensitive studies, I think you will realise that the myriad lines and folds present on hands are not a necessary feature of the carving. I left my carving with a tooled finish to indicate the textured surface of the skin. In contrast, the egg was finely sanded and polished.

The anatomical studies illustrated are not intended to educate anyone in the mysteries of physiology, but merely to indicate the amazing complexity of this unique tool. Bear this in mind when you are carving it, and it will add something to the sculpture.

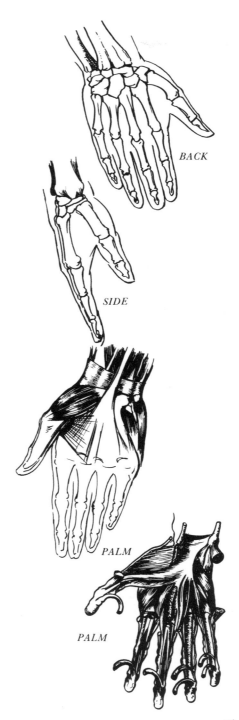

BACK

SIDE

PALM

PALM

Figure 130

Figure 131

Figure 132

24   "Mother" from *Cider with Rosie*

Here is a sculpture based on a literary character from Laurie Lee's famous book *Cider with Rosie*. There are literally thousands of instances when the carver can guess at or imagine the strong points of character that go to make a striking personality from the world of novels, plays and poetry. Indeed, there are, later in this book, some used from *Alice in Wonderland* and *Winnie the Pooh*, but the list is endless as a source of subject matter and one that is only briefly touched on here.

I thought it would be nice to include this 'portrait' in this section as the photographic model is the actress Josephine Tewson who was playing the part in a production of the play at The Everyman Theatre in Cheltenham. What is important here is to get the feeling of the character and the period, through the costume and 'presence' of the actress.

Aiming for true likeness when working from photographs is obviously very difficult indeed. The photograph is too remote and impersonal and one is bound to rely on characteristics, rather than actual features.

In this study the top half of the figure is very busy so I decided to make the skirt plain and severe. Typical garments of this type are readily available and should be studied. The hat is something else again. In the photograph it is covered with flowers, presumably aritificial, and appears to have ostrich feathers hanging over the side. On this scale, I didn't think feathers would really work very well so I substituted a piece of fabric. The hanging piece is very delicate so I left it uncarved until the rest of the figure was polished. The wicker basket is quite easily accomplished using a 1mm No. 11 gouge.

Figure 133

Figure 134

Figure 135

Figure 136

Figure 137

25 China Figure

Figure 138

This carving has two benefits: firstly, it entirely eliminates research, and secondly, it is an excellent exercise in understanding the work of another artist.

Most households have a few china ornaments in the shape of animals, people etc., and provided they are of reasonable quality, it is fair to assume that the man who made the original had considerable ability. When you are going to cast thousands of copies, you can afford to have the original made properly.

I am not, therefore, suggesting that you copy this figure, although the reference material is here, but find your own and commence in the usual way with a detailed measured drawing, followed by the bandsawn shape. Drawing the plans should present no problem, since the figure can be measured as much as required.

The carving is straightforward enough, but a certain amount of rethinking will be necessary. Moulded clay has its own limitations. You will find no sharp edges or sharp grooves; undercutting is almost non-existent and everything is softly and smoothly modelled. Much of the detail, such as eyes, lips, and so on, is only suggested in the form, the shape being painted on subsequently. Exceptions to this will be found in certain types of Capo di Monte and other fine porcelain sculptures. This is a valuable exercise and invariably produces a good carving.

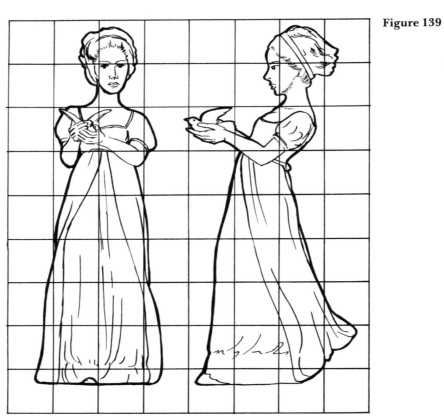

Figure 139

Figure 140

Figure 141

Figure 142

Figure 143

26 Head of Alexander the Great

Figure 144

This is a very difficult carving; classical heads were not conceived by 20th century minds and the philosophy underlying the distortions and characteristics of the classical Greek features are alien to me. Added to the fact that only one view of the original stone carving was available and the head has no nose or top lip, the piece becomes more a process of decision-making than carving. For this reason I decided to make a full-size clay model first (see Fig. 146). This is always a useful process but not one I always adopt. It is very time consuming but its value in figure carving to those who have difficulty in 'seeing' the shape to be cut away is enormous.

Carving the actual features of the face requires patience and accurate measurement. The skin surface is painstakingly sanded and polished and the hair left from the chisel. The process of carving the hair can be seen in Figures 148 to 150. Having roughed out the dome of the head, the main lines of the hair are drawn on it. These lines are now deeply incised with a "V" chisel and then softened with a flat gouge.

Figure 145

Figure 146

Figure 147

100

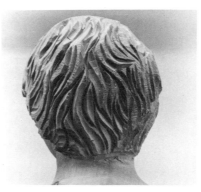

Figure 148

Figure 149

Figure 150

Figure 151

Figure 152

ARTISANS AT WORK

Figure 153

27 Stonemason

I have carved quite a few craftsmen at work and I suppose that is because people like them. I think the pleasure in watching someone else working is widespread and extends into making or possessing a sculpture of a workman.

I intended, originally, to have my stonemason stood before a half-finished piece of work, but I felt that the chisel and mallet poised over a virgin block of stone gave a feeling of anticipation and impetus – one can share a feeling of creativity with the mason as the razor-sharp steel is about to cut into the soft limestone of the Cotswolds; he is waiting to hear the thump of the mallet.

My model was more a stonewaller than a mason, in fact, and they don't seem to wear old aprons and have knarled hands and wrinkled nut-brown faces anymore.

Boxwood is not particularly necessary for a carving of this scale: sycamore, lime, or fruit-wood would be equally satisfactory, but I find that the beauty and quality of box makes you try harder, for the sake of the wood. It is worthy of your best effort. I made the mallet and chisel separately but it's not necessary if you prefer to work in the solid. The block is separate because I wanted it really square and flat.

Figure 154

Figure 155

Figure 156

Figure 157

Figure 158

Figure 159

28 Dry-Stonewaller

Figure 160

This study of an old tradesman was done specifically to epitomise the Cotswolds, and a photograph of it was used to publicise an exhibition entitled "Cotswold Images".

Obviously, you can only have a small piece of wall, but the big decision is how much. I think the answer lies in your concept of the piece as a work of art. If the wall was removed completely, the figure alone would then be seen as a portrait of an individual who happens to be a stonewaller. On the other hand if there is a large portion of wall and surrounding grass, stones, etc., so that the figure is part of a landscape, it becomes more of a tableau, the man's individuality subordinate to the scene. I originally had more wall than is shown and a tree stump, but I gradually cut pieces away and removed the tree until I had the balance I required.

The impression I wanted to convey was of a particular person at a precise moment in time: he pauses in his work when a sound catches his attention – perhaps the report of a shotgun or a hunting horn – and he is frozen, eyes searching the horizon.

There are no special difficulties with this piece other than acquiring the reference material to carve from. For this purpose I recruited a model, and having suitably attired and equipped him, I took photographs from all four sides. Although one or two details, such as the hat and shoes were subsequently altered and the face of an actual stonewaller transplanted, the naturalness of the pose and the hang of the clothes provide the basis of the carving. Sections of stone wall were also photographed and a few pieces of Cotswold stone acquired for closer study. The face and arms and the stone were left with a tooled finish to create a kind of bond between the man and the stone. His clothes were sanded.

Figure 161

Figure 162

Figure 163

Figure 164　Cotswold stone waiting for a wall.

Figure 165　Dry-stone wall in need of the stonewaller.

Figure 166

29   The Blacksmith

It would be nice to find a really hulking great blacksmith like the late Joe Price of Gloucester, who could write on a blackboard with a 56lb weight hanging from his little finger; but any blacksmith is hard to find, especially those whose physique is expected to form part of the craft folklore. I used a friend as a model and obtained details from a book.

The carving is fairly straightforward although a large piece of wood is needed, especially if the anvil is to be part of the block.

In this model you will see from the drawings that the figure and anvil are connected only by the tongs and horse-shoe and as such allows the choice of using two smaller pieces of wood or, more importantly, a change of timber to effect the difference between the blacksmith and his anvil.

The hammer and the tongs holding the horse-shoe are the obvious difficulties. The best system is to start at the outer extremity, i.e. the hammer head, and work down to the hand, completely finishing it as you go.

The sketches of the boot and rolled-up sleeve could be used as useful practice pieces before commencing any artisan model. They form the basis of authentic and natural detail which could be applied to many sculptures.

Figure 167

Figure 168

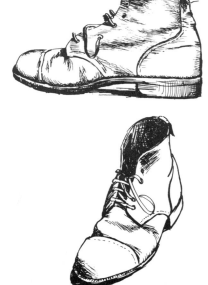

Figure 169

Figure 170

Figure 171

MUSICIANS

Figure 172

30　The Cellist

This piece was suggested by the painting of *Madame Suggia* by Augustus John and of which I have tried to make a representation in ink.

What I liked was the archetypal pose and air of the painting, though I didn't want to use the actual woman. I persuaded a friend to pose for me holding a thin cross-frame to put his limbs in the right position, but enabling me to see what was behind the cello. I then took pictures from all four sides.

This is a difficult carving involving some highly detailed features, considerable amounts of folded drapery of the typical uniform of a virtuoso, and very precise constructional work. Also, the measurements must be very precise indeed and the organisation of stages most carefully worked out.

The first step after bandsawing, assuming that, like mine, your wood is inadequate dimensionally, is to glue the arm on. The carving can then be roughed out. However the space between the knees must be accurately measured and marked to accept the cello. It follows that the

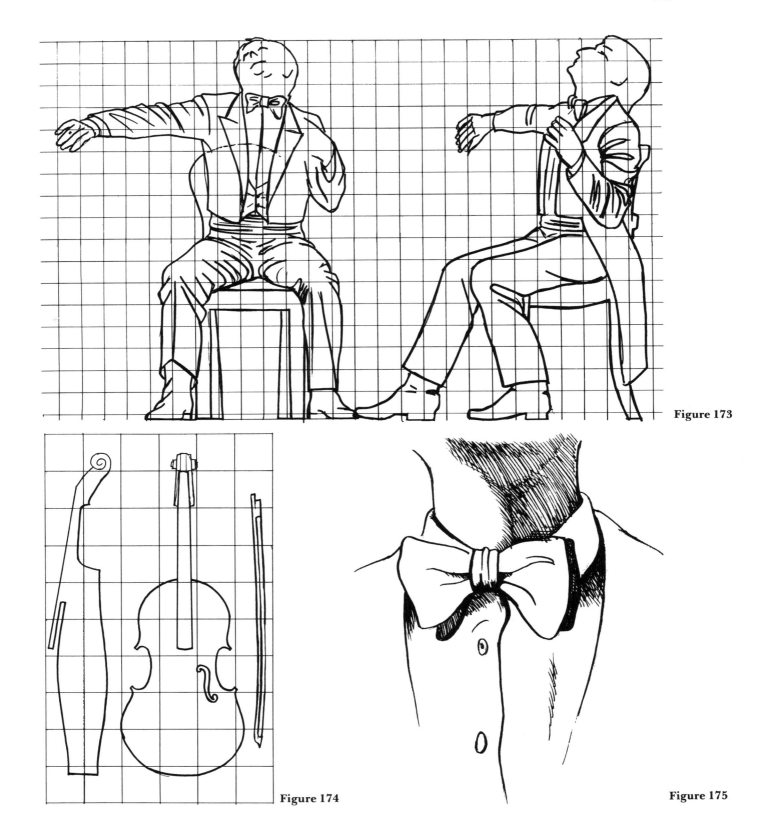

Figure 173

Figure 174

Figure 175

body of the cello is best cut out at the same time as the figure. (Do not at this time reduce the size of the chair legs to their finished size as they must take the strain of the work). The hand fingering the instrument must also be cut fairly accurately so that it will hold the neck quite tightly. Once it is established that the cello fits into place, carving can proceed normally. Coming to the hand holding the bow, use a strip of wood to get the correct position of the hand relating to the strings.

Making the instrument is a delicate job. The body and neck are carved from the solid. The head is then drilled to take the pegs which are turned and carved to push in as in the real instrument. The bridge is carved with two small tenons at the bottom which fit into appropriate mortises in the face of the cello. The fishtail has a small tab at right angles in the lower end and two small steel pins are inserted to hold it strongly in position. The long spike which rests on the floor is turned and glued into a drilled hole in the body. The strings, which are cotton are glued to the tensioning pegs and knotted through holds drilled in the fishtail. The pegs are then turned until the cotton is tightened. The bow is carved minus the hair which is imitated by a strip cut from a thickly planed shaving.

Taken steadily, a piece at a time, it is perhaps, less difficult than it first seems.

Figure 177

Figure 178

Figure 179

Figure 176

Figure 180

31   The Violinist

Figure 181

The Violinist is based on a piece from a collection of gypsy music – the slow passages stretched out, as if the record has slowed down – the musician, tall and lean, as one with the music.

I made a few sketches to put down my ideas, then worked up a clay model. It was actually at this stage I decided to incorporate the curves of the treble-clef into the line of the figure.

This requires eliminating unnecessary detail, so the treatment of the clothing is fairly simple. Fig. 181 shows how the whole figure is based in a long curve sweeping from the floor up the near leg and chest following the axis of the head. The line of the front leg runs up the back of the body and head. This can be seen again in Fig. 185 where the line of the near leg is taken up in the folds of the shirt. From the back Fig. 186, the figure is stiff and straight. The coat from any view, winds and flows around this basic bow

Figure 182

shape. These flowing lines are repeated in the hair, the shape of the violin and the folds in the clothes.

The carving itself is not too difficult. The instrument could have been made separately but was not; the bow was made by the same method as that of the cellist. Details such as the hands, were obtained from books on violin fingering.

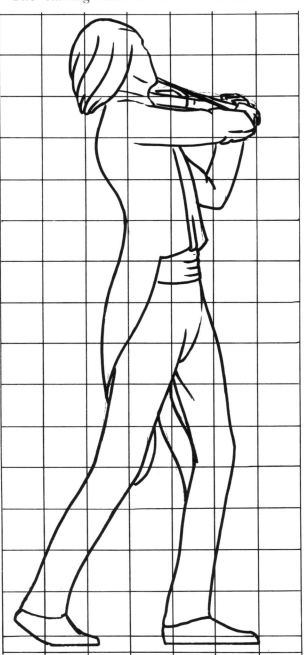
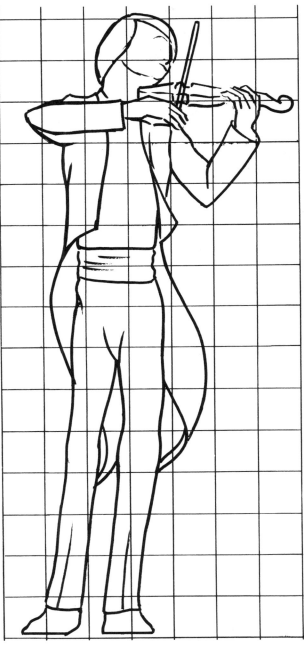

Figure 183

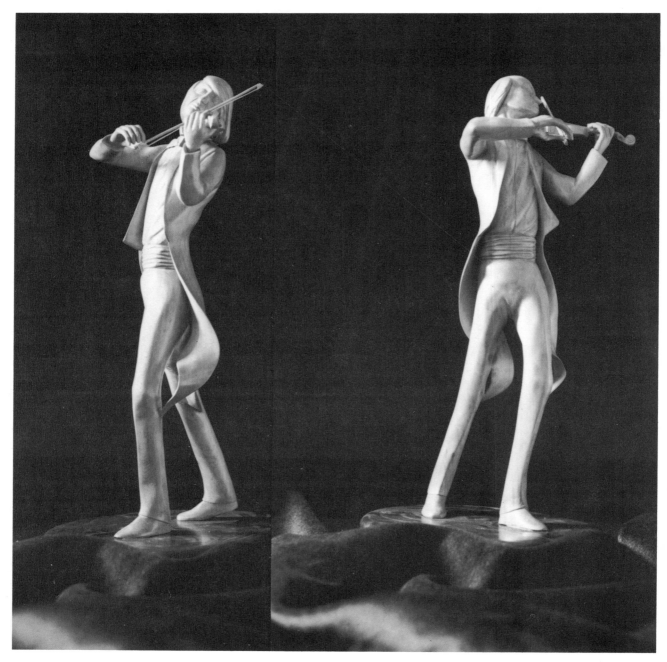

Figures 184 & 185

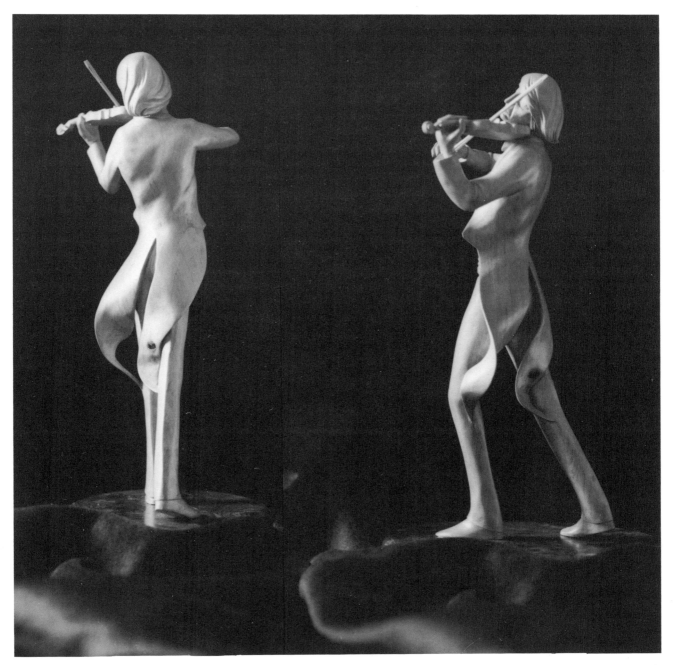

Figures 186 & 187

32 The Bagpiper

Figure 188

The works of artists of the past provide a rich source of ideas for carvers. There is, of course, no need to adhere rigidly to the painting, after all the painter is more interested in colour than form, and what may look good on canvas could well be uncarvable or uninteresting in wood.

Pieter Bruegel is well-known for the multitude of figures in his pictures, mostly peasants going about their daily lives and performing every conceivable task. They are depicted accurately and clearly, details of costume and accessories can readily be observed.

The bagpipes is a very old instrument and appears in many of his works and the figure I have based my carving on is from *Wedding Dance in the Open Air* now in the Detroit Institute of Arts, but I have used information from several others as well.

Bruegel's figures appear uniformly overweight in a curious way, and they wear heavy puffed-out clothes, giving them a kind of inflated appearance. I think it is important to try and capture this feeling in the wood. I used maple because it is fairly plain but achieves a fine hard surface, and here is more suitable than lime.

The carving is quite straightforward with some difficult cutting between the bagpipes and the body. The pipes are turned (although they could of course be carved with some difficulty) and inserted into two holes drilled between the bagpipes and the body. I left them unglued to facilitate transport and polishing. The mouthpiece is carved and glued into a groove in the bagpipes neck and a hole in the mouth. Maple requires very careful and thorough sanding, and being hard, I would recommend a high quality abrasive such as open coat aluminium oxide paper or cloth, or silicon carbide. On light coloured woods I find that cellulose sealer is better then shellac, being completely colourless.

Figure 189   **Figure 190**   **Figure 191**

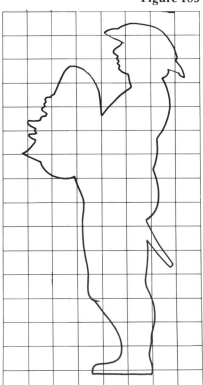
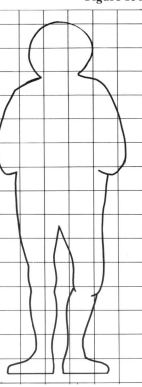
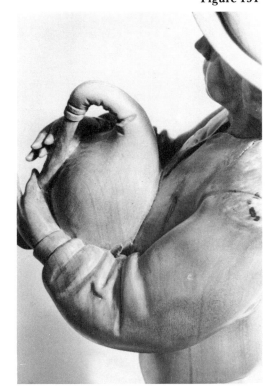

Figure 192

33   The Lutist

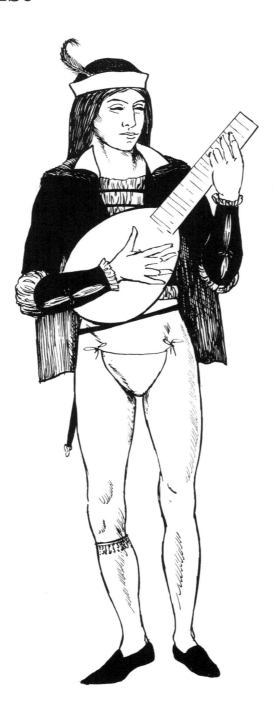

Figure 193

The costume for the lute player was taken from a book on the subject which also explained the styles, fabrics and functions of the various garments. I have altered some of it; the cloak, for instance, should be attached to the elbow of the doublet, and I have omitted a piece of lace usually worn around the knee. The face is based on a portrait painted by the Florentine artist Botticelli, and details of the lute can be obtained easily from research at the public library, (or it can easily be changed for a guitar or mandolin for your own project).

Although there may be some difficulty under-cutting around the back of the instrument, the carving is fairly straightforward.

Figure 194

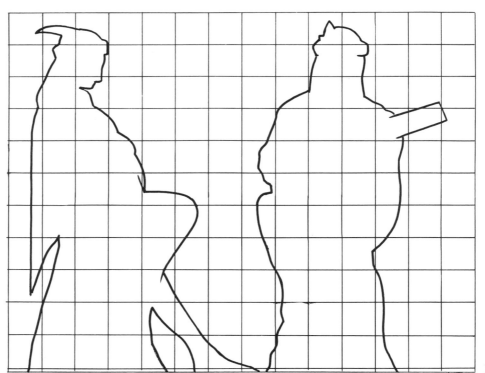

Figure 195

Figures 196 & 197

34 The Pied Piper

Figure 198

This figure is based on Arthur Rackham's illustrations for Browning's famous poem. The drawings are not very clear so my original sketch uses a good deal of artistic licence. This is a very good example where it is a great help with a carving of this type, to make a clay model. Thin waving strips of cloth cannot easily be drawn accurately and it is even more difficult to visualise them three-dimensionally.

Olivewood is very expensive but carves beautifully, and its erratic streaking, I felt, emphasised the movement without obscuring the forms. The pipe music I had in mind was lively and fast, rather like an Irish reel. I wanted everything in the figure to be on the move and I have tried to have every limb at a different angle, every piece of cloth waving and flapping, but at the same time, by repeating shapes and curves, to imbue a rhythm into the whole.

It is a difficult carving by any standards but not as time consuming as one might think. It is more a case of you've cut it right or you're picking up pieces off the floor – it's rather nerve-racking. The easiest way to carve the thin pieces of cloth is to cut the most inaccessible side first and then shape the outside to match the inside. The legs, being very thin, must be left till last.

Probably the greatest difficulty experienced will be in fitting the pipe and carving the hands. When the hands and the knot of the scarf attached to the pipe are roughly carved, Fig. 205, drill a hole through them to the mouth. Insert an odd piece of wood (I used an old paint brush) fairly tightly through the holes. This will strengthen the three parts and give you a guide to fit the fingers. When the figure is completely finished, the pipe, turned from ebony, can be fitted.

Figures 199 & 200

Figure 201

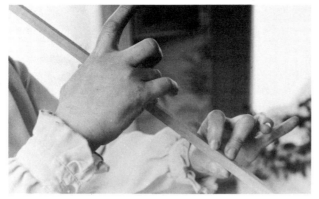

Figure 202

Figure 203

Figure 204

Figure 205

Figure 206

Figure 207

Figure 208

STORYBOOK CHARACTERS

Figure 209

35 A Favourite Bear

This might seem a very silly carving but he is the idol of all young children and many adults, and it does pose an interesting problem of textures for the carver. I think if I were carving only a teddy bear on this scale I would give it a smooth finish, but in this situation the jar has to have the smooth finish; so where does that leave the teddy bear? I plumped for a finely tooled finish using a 6mm No. 7 gouge.

A rather unpleasant dead knot appeared inside the wood by the right ear, which had to be partly filled and painted over with coloured french polish. A few spirit stains and some prepared powder pigments can be a very useful adjunct to the carver's equipment.

The lettering on the jar, which is very shallow, was done with a 4mm spoon bent macaroni tool.

I think, the key to this carving is, perhaps, to shape the jar accurately from the drawings and fit the bear to it.

Figure 210

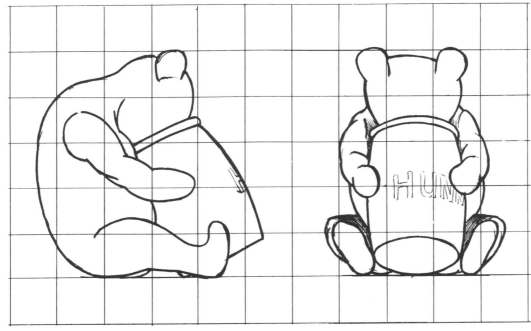

Figure 211

Figure 212

36 Officer of the Court (from *Alice in Wonderland*)

This little figure is not as easy as it might at first appear. The illustration, copied from the Tenniel original, does not tell us a great deal, so we must surmise what the missing information is.

The caricatured face can be made up from what is shown in the illustration, and the front view created by laterally transferring the features on the drawing. A suitable length for the tunic must be decided and the position of the feet and legs. I chose the bandy legs and the 'ten-to-two' feet, but he might equally be knock-kneed and pigeon-toed.

The wood I chose, bubinga, I had never carved before, and whilst I would not complain of its carving qualities, its colour tends to look as though it is badly stained with red polish.

Figure 213

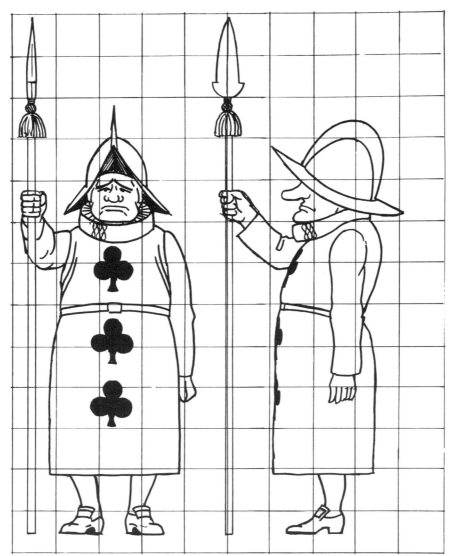

Figure 214

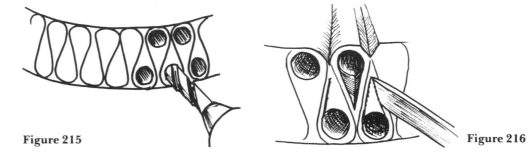

Figure 215

Figure 216

The spear is made in two parts: the head is turned and pared down to form the blade, leaving the bell shaped tassel to be textured with the V tool; the shaft is a sawn 3/16″ (4mm) square rod, subsequently rounded on a drum sander. I find this is better than turned shafts, which always look like dowelling. It is then inserted through a drilled hole in the hand.

The "clubs" on the front of his tunic were first incised to the depth of ⅛″ (3mm) then filled by melting black sealing wax into them which is smoothed off with a hot knife.

An interesting detail is the ruff round the collar. This was formed from folded linen, creating tear-drop shaped tubes. To create this appearance first carve the ruff as a flat disc and mark out the teardrop shapes; then drill a 1/16″ (1.5mm) hole into each shape, using a ¼″ (6mm) No. 2 to cut away the vee-shaped chip to complete the tear drop. See Figs. 215 and 216.

Figure 217

37   Hatta in Prison (from *Alice in Wonderland*)

This is a similar study to the Office of the Court but more difficult, both technically and artistically. Obviously these two factors overlap, but there is an enormous amount of careful undercutting to be done around the legs of the stool, the feet and the arms, that is difficult and rather tedious.

The most troublesome part of all where more aesthetic decision-making is needed is in the face. Fortunately, Tenniel has produced several draw-ings of the Mad Hatter, and his reincarnation Hatta, and it is possible with a little research to obtain an accurate profile. With precise band-sawing, this means that we can produce a perfect outline on the carving giving us a basis to create the finished head.

It is difficult to achieve the anxious look of the original illustration rather than a frightened or startled expression. The problem is in the eyes. I

Figure 218

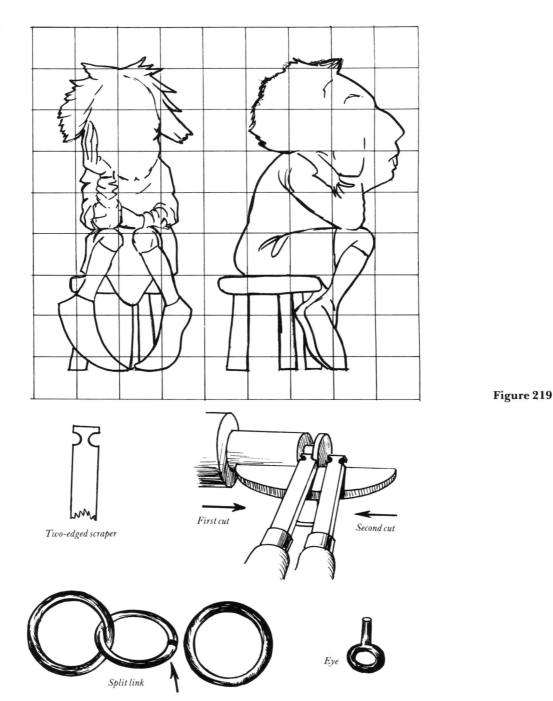

Figure 219

Two-edged scraper

First cut　　　*Second cut*

Figure 220

Making the Chain

Split link　　　*Eye*

The links are turned on the lathe. The cutter can be ground from **thin silver steel rod, ⅛″ × ¼″.** The wood is turned to a cylinder and **a deep** cut, slightly wider than the cutter, is made, one ring thickness from the end. One side of the cutter is then applied to the inside edge of the ring blank, then the other side of the cutter to the outside edge. When the cuts meet, the ring comes free. Some sanding may be necessary on the inside edge.

have recessed the iris, but the expression tends to depend on the way the light catches this recess. The hair is roughly tooled to look untidy and dishevelled.

Both the hat and the pillar were roughly turned to shape, the hat being finished by the normal process of carving, and the pillar merely cleaned up on a sanding drum.

Finally, the chain was made from African blackwood, the links being turned rings and the eye in the wall, carved.

Every alternate ring is split on one side, and the two adjacent unsplit rings fed into it, finally gluing the joint. The leg ring is made in a similar fashion to slip over the foot.

I found that the holly I used had little to recommend it as a carving timber. It certainly was not white, and was very hard and stringy. Sycamore or maple would undoubtedly be a better choice.

Figure 221

38   Toad on the
Barge Horse (from *Wind in the Willows*)

Figure 222

There is a subtle difference between the animal caricatures of Tenniel in *Alice in Wonderland* and those of Rackham in *The Wind in the Willows*. Tenniel's animals are presented as animals that speak, whereas Rackham's are a complete blend of animal and human. The toad, for example, is of human size and is capable of masquerading as a washerwoman. He has a human body and voice; only his head and hands are those of a toad. This, therefore, presents the carver with the problem of making a figure of a woman in a frilly dress and hat, which must be immediately recognisable as a dressed up toad. If the audience has to ask what it is the carving loses all impact. Another consideration is the horse – it has the look of a caricature, but on closer examination it becomes clear that it is in fact a skilled drawing of a rather old, broken-down horse, displaying the typical bony hips, curly hooves and knobbly knees of the type.

Normally, I carve a horse separately from the base which greatly facilitates the work, enabling the legs to be bandsawn away. In this case I felt that since the horse is eating the grass, it should be an integral part of the carving. This adds considerably to the work involved and takes

Figure 223

plenty of patience to carve the inside surfaces.

The hat is a problem, I could find nothing quite like it to refer to. It appears to be simply a bundle of pieces of ribbon. I decided to carve the outside edge as a series of V tool cuts and the top surface as a multitude of shallow gouge cuts, using a ¼″ (6mm) No. 5 simply pushed into the wood at about 45° and taken out without removing a chip, then another similar cut made immediately behind it. Repeating this in concentric circles leaves numerous thin flakes of wood standing up.

The wooden cylinder hanging on the horse's rump was simply whittled from an offcut. The knots at the end of the rope were carved as part of this. The knots at the other end were carved as part of the harness. The ropes themselves were whittled from strips of wood sawn to shape, the ends glued into holes drilled in the knots.

The timber used, field maple, looks similar to lime or sycamore, but is very hard and not a particularly pleasant wood in which to carve fine detail. Despite its difficulties, however, it takes a beautiful polish and has a quality superior to lime for this type of subject.

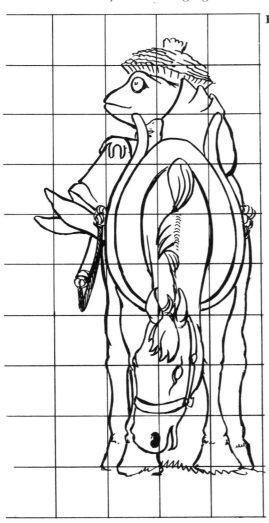

Figure 224

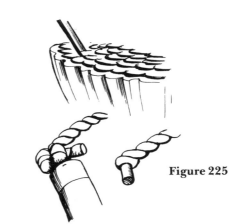

Figure 225

Detail of cutting for hat and detail of rope and harness

Figure 226

Figure 227

39 Lion & Unicorn (from *Alice in Wonderland*)

Figure 228

The Lion and the Unicorn are, in my opinion, along with the White Knight, Tenniel's best characterisations in *Alice in Wonderland* and *Through the Looking Glass*. They are the only ones I have carved twice; the second version being slightly altered from the original.

One assumes that there are political overtones to the drawing which are not in the text. The unicorn is dressed as a Spanish grandee – swaggering, arrogant and bullying. The lion, on the other hand, is a doddering old gentleman. His coat appears to be a sort of pantomime suit hanging in baggy folds round his knees. He peers myopically at the unicorn, holding his *pince-nez* and looking as if he is about to collapse. Yet the story tells us that he beat the unicorn all around the town. Be that as it may, the pair present ideal subjects for character carvings.

I carved the originals in cherry and teak and the second ones in boxwood and walnut. The cherry was, I think, better than the box in effect, because the streaks in the grain helped to create the feeling of flashy clothes. For the lion, the walnut is easier to carve and more effective.

The only difficult parts of these figures are the unicorn's ruff, described in the 'Officer of the Court' (see Fig. 215), the unicorn's horn and the lion's spectacles. The horn is carved separately. If you want to make the spiral accurate, cut a long thin strip of paper and wind it around the horn, see Fig. 229, which will create a spiral where the layers overlap. Cut through the line with a sharp knife to mark the wood underneath.

The spectacles are made of ebony in one figure and box in the other. I drilled the hole before cutting out the shape with a fret-saw, they were then filed and sanded. They are very, very fragile. I also made the unicorn's buttons separately and pegged them in.

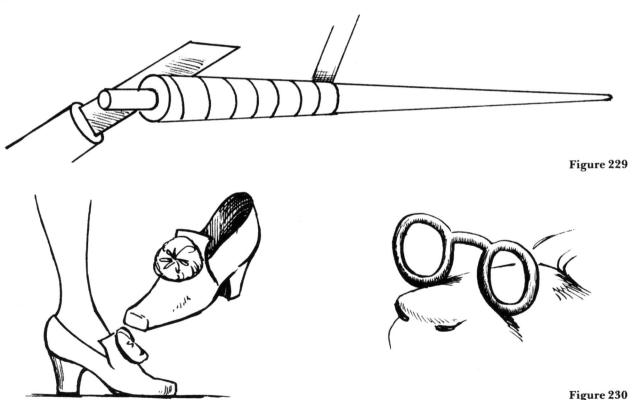

Figure 229

Figure 230

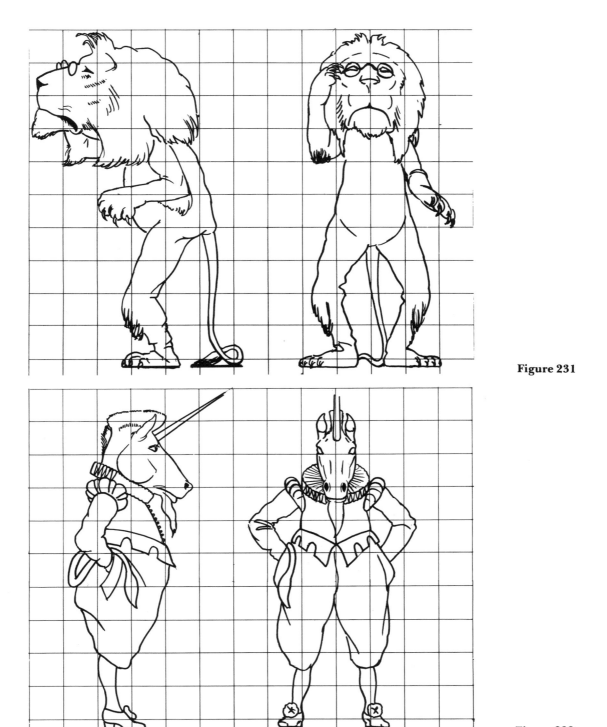

Figure 231

Figure 232

Figure 233 Original carving in cherry and teak.

Figure 234 Second carving in boxwood and walnut.

40 Red Dragon of Wales

Figure 235

In 1536 Henry VIII completed the gardens of Hampton Court Palace. In honour of the Queen, Anne Boleyn, he erected twelve carved stone statues of heraldic animals on the parapet of the bridge over the moat. These figures eventually succumbed to the rigours of time and fell into the moat – parts of them being excavated in 1909, when new figures were made to replace the originals. Unfortunately, the new statues lasted only until 1950 when they again needed replacing, this time by the figures to be seen adorning the bridge at present. The dragon, one of the most interesting of the beasts, symbolises the royal Welsh ancestry of the Tudor dynasty.

The dragon is carved in red padauk, a brilliant red wood which carves well, leaving clean, shining toolcuts. The front surface of the shield should be formed first leaving the claws standing above it. The shield must be accurately shaped, whereas the body can be altered somewhat, so it is best to establish its outline and thickness then shape the body to fit it. Cutting away the space behind the shield is a difficult, tedious job, but produces a far better effect than if it is left solid. The scales require careful cutting and sharp chisels if the edges are not to crumble. The mouth is pierced right through, between the teeth and tongue. I used dental burrs in a hand-set but small gouges could be used. The painting of the Welsh Dragon on the shield is not what everyone would want and it requires very careful, patient work with enamels.

Padauk takes an excellent wax polish without sealing. The wood subsequently darkens to a deep red.

Figure 236

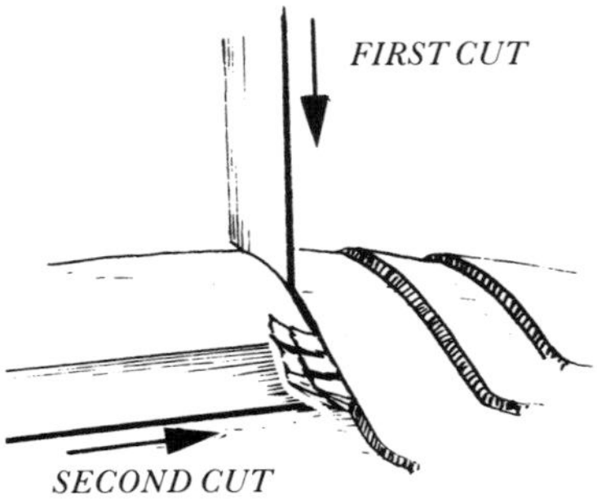

Figure 236

Figure 237   Cutting the scales.

Figure 238   Cutting the eye.

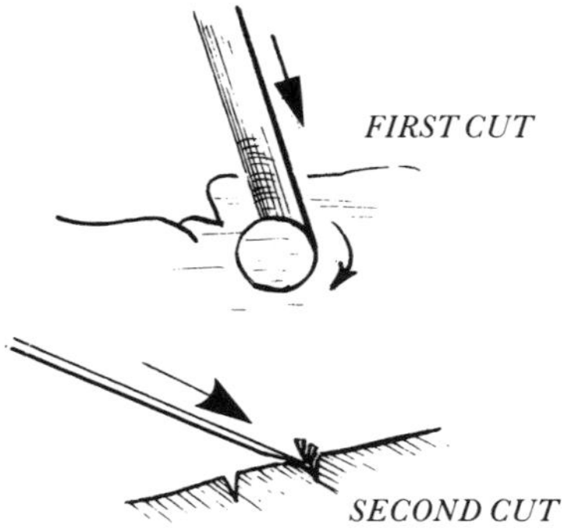

Figure 239

CARVINGS TO USE

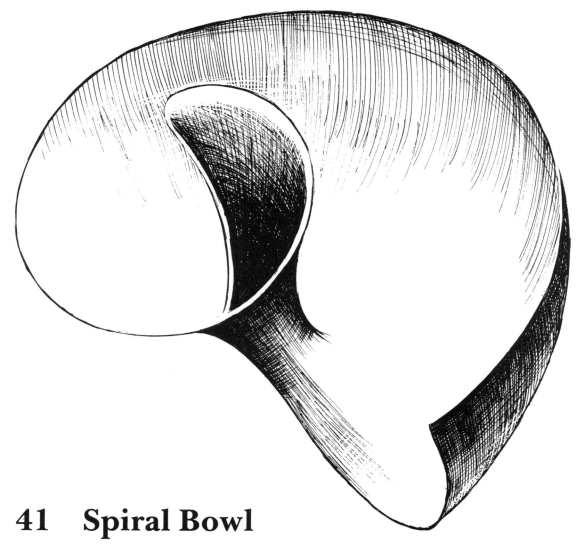

41   Spiral Bowl

Figure 240

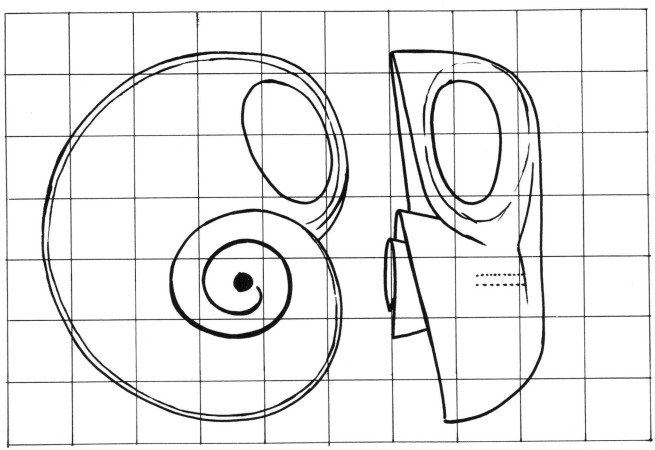

Figure 241

Having dealt with spirals and shells in some detail in the "Snail" project it occurred to me that halving a carved shell would make a serving container of sorts. To make a bowl of reasonable size required a fairly large piece of timber, but the turning blanks sold by timber dealers are ideal. The wild grain of yew wood is ideal but its tendency to faultiness makes the choice of a suitable piece difficult.

The underside must be shaped first and this can be done either by holding the piece with a holdfast or G-cramp or screwing it to a block and holding it in the vice. I roughed out the bottom with a gouge and smoothed it off with a rasp.

To hold the block to carve the top surface it is necessary to locate the centre of the spiral underneath and insert a heavy screw to hold a block, or use a carver's screw. The carving of the upper surface is easy enough if you have a few spoon gouges. Great care must be taken to ensure that the curves are smooth and even and that the line of the spiral is flat in the horizontal view. The central coil actually rises considerably higher than on my carving but this is dependent on the thickness of wood available.

The designed loop-hole that is swept up acts both as a partial restraint for the contents and as a natural handling end leaving in free view the

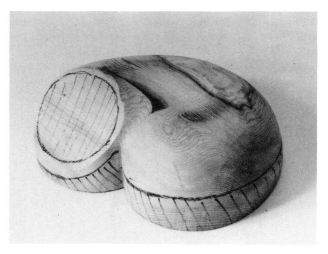

Figure 242

Figure 243

tighter spiralling coil.

As always with smooth flowing lines and curves, the finish must be immaculate and that can involve an enormous effort of sanding. However, in this case, some of the work can be assisted by the use of rotary sanders. Various sizes of flap wheel are available, which, fitted in an electric drill or flexible drive shaft, can be used to sand much of the inside curves (Fig. 244).

A foam drum sander mounted on a motor or drill stand will likewise smooth most of the outside surface as in Fig. 245. Hand finishing will of course be necessary, particularly around the centre spiral, which later is drilled almost to the bottom.

The finished bowl was given several coats of cellulose sealer, rubbed down with fine steel wool and polished.

Figure 244

Figure 245

Figure 246

42   Jewellery

I suppose most woodworkers have a box somewhere, full of small pieces of beautiful wood that they do not want to throw away but have no use for. I, in fact, used the offcuts of Mexican rosewood from the snake carving and a piece of African blackwood that was cut from the base of an heraldic bull to make these odd items of jewellery. It is very pleasant sometimes, to make something that costs nothing in materials and is finished in a couple of hours, instead of days, and that you feel you can simply give to someone. I think the field is wide open for the use of wood as jewellery and other similar adornments, such as buckles and buttons, etc.

I chose beetles partly because they were used for jewellery in the past and also because insects tend to be neglected in art. We are quite happy to reduce an elephant to a six inch carving, but one rarely sees a tiny insect enlarged to six inches.

Carving the brooch and pendant is very straightforward. Leave some extra thickness of wood underneath if you want to hold the piece in the vice, although it could well be done with a knife, hand held. The eyes of the pendant are turned ebony pegs glued in, and the chain passes through the hole bored in the back of the head. For the purposes envisaged here I felt that the legs and feelers were superfluous.

The bracelet is more difficult. It is primarily turned on the lathe in the form of a plain flattish ring, no real attempt being made to finish the surface. The tapering shape is then cut either by hand or on the bandsaw, and all the surface filed flat. I say filed, because blackwood is a lot easier to file than cut. It is then fairly straightforward to cut and file the shapes of the beetles in the block that is left. Careful sanding and polishing is all that remains. Jewellery fittings are readily available from craft shops.

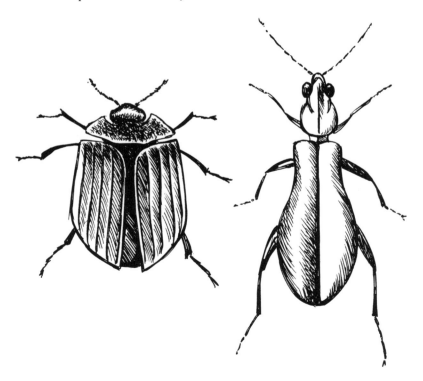

Figure 247

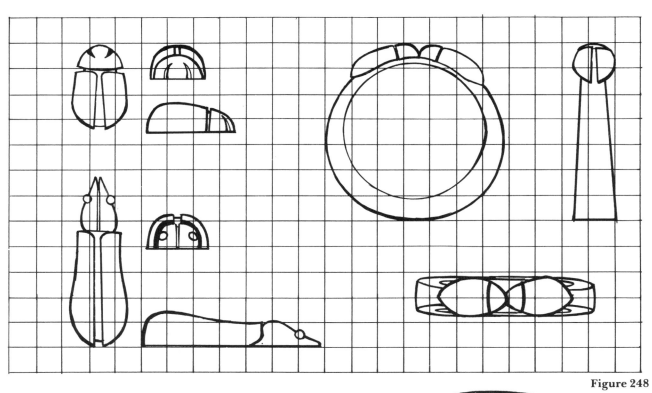

Figure 248

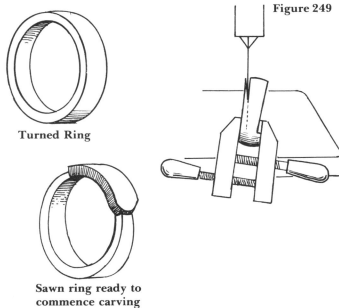

Figure 249

Turned Ring

Sawn ring ready to
commence carving

Note It is most important that the ring is held in a clamp for bandsawing or a serious accident will occur. *This warning should not be taken lightly.*

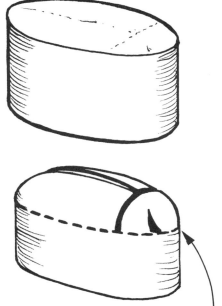

Figure 250 Bandsawn block for brooch. This can be held in the vice and sawn off when finished.

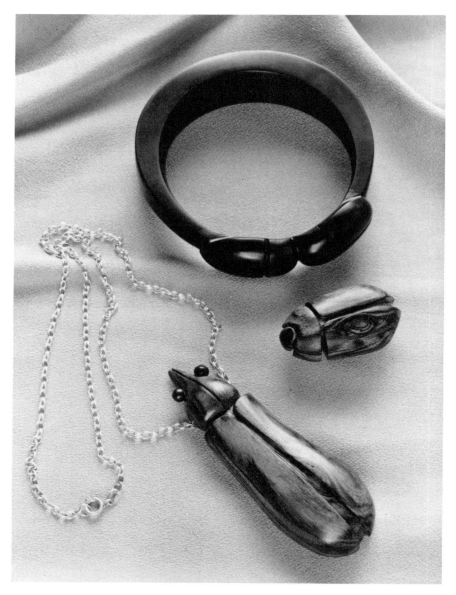

Figure 251

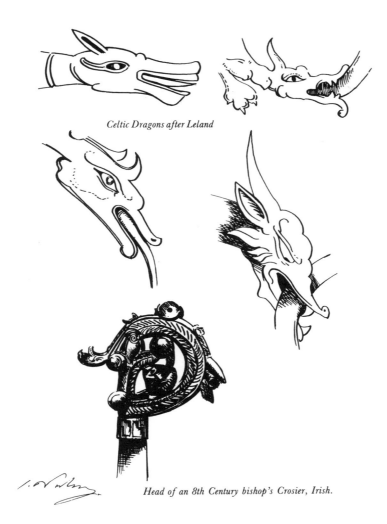

Celtic Dragons after Leland

Head of an 8th Century bishop's Crosier, Irish.

Figure 252

43   Walking Stick

It is always interesting to work within the parameters dictated by the intended use of an object, and the discipline involved in producing works of art in this way has given the world some of its finest pieces.

A walking stick handle must comfortably fit the hand, have no fragile protusions and obviously be limited to the size of the stick at the lower end. Within these guidelines your imagination can have free rein. The celtic style of art has always interested me and Charles Leland's book *Woodcarving* contains a great wealth of it.

The head of the dragon could be used the other way round, the neck becoming the stick, but I liked the idea of the flames from the beast's mouth wrapping themselves around the ebony.

Having bandsawn the head and flames, from one side only, the next step is to bore a ¾" (19mm) hole into it, up as far as the first teeth. See Fig. 254. Next bore a ⅜" (10mm) hole from

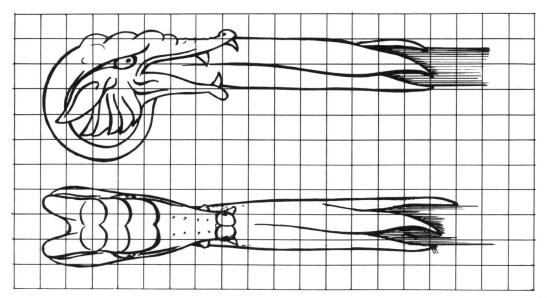

Figure 253

Figure 255

Figure 254

Figure 256

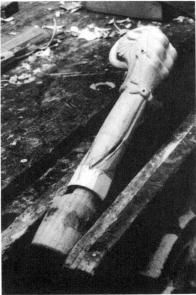

the bottom of the first hole into the head up to the eyes. This is to accept a steel rod which will penetrate a similar distance into the ebony. The ebony cane was turned on the lathe – not the easiest task – and completely sanded and polished. One end was turned to fit into the handle and a ⅜″ (10mm) hole drilled into its end about 3″ (75mm) deep to accept the steel rod.

For the carving of the head the square stem with the ¾″ (19mm) hole is quite strong enough to hold in the vice. The carving is straightforward and could be left straight from the chisel although mine was sanded. The wood I used, hawthorn, is very fine to work and takes a beautiful polish. The pupils of the eyes and the nostrils are deeply drilled holes. When the head is completely finished, turn a dummy walking stick to fit the hole, see Fig. 256, a few inches long, and you can then carve the flames while this dummy is held in the vice.

With the carving completed, glue in the steel rod and ebony cane with epoxy resin. Rubber tips of various designs and sizes are readily available.

Figure 257

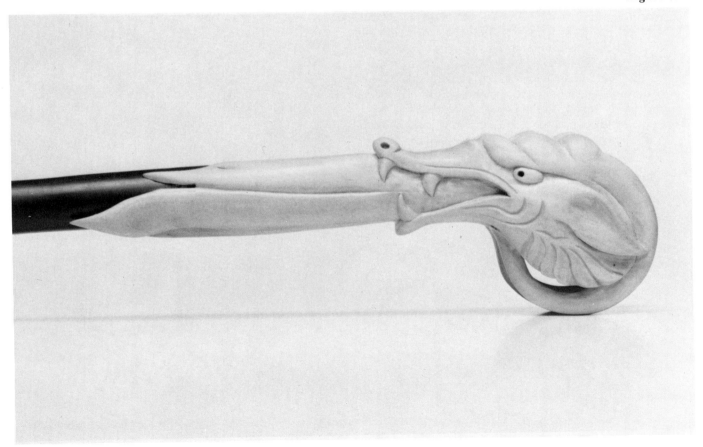

44 Pipe

Carved pipes are as old as smoking itself and the skill and workmanship that has been expended on some of the finer examples is quite staggering. Many of the best carved pipes were meerschaum rather than wood because this material was considered to have the best smoking qualities, and was excellent to carve. Nowadays, briar is the popular timber for pipes. This is the root of a bush that grows in the south of France and is of a pink colour, burry in texture and quite dense. It is pleasant to carve, taking very fine detail and a fine polish. Blanks, ready bored and complete with stem, are available from pipe-making companies for a small sum.

The immediate problem is holding the blank whilst it is carved and this is simply solved by making a tight fitting plug, in the place where the tobacco bowl will be, which can be held in the vice. This gives greater versatility and accessibility for the work (see Figs. 260 and 261).

The aesthetic considerations warrant some thought. You may or may not be a pipe smoker but the habits of them are well-known. The pipe is held by the thumb, forefinger and index finger with which they continuously fondle the thing. The tactile qualities of the pipe are therefore

Figure 258

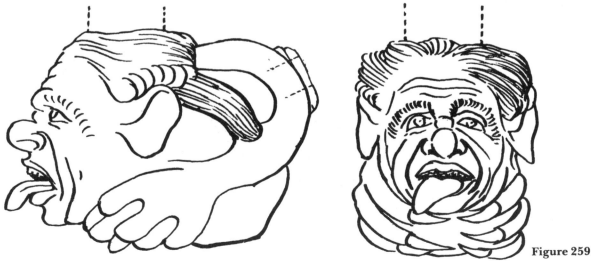

Figure 259

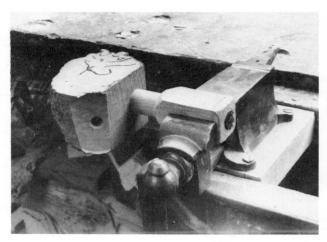

Figure 260

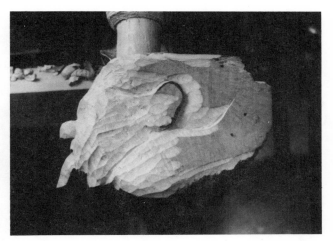

Figure 261

important. It seems to me that a variety of surfaces are needed: smooth polished curves, finely tooled sections, and hollows which the fingers would settle in.

A head is, of course, a natural subject for a pipe, since it lends itself to the restrictions of the shape. The design I have used is taken from a mediaeval stone carving, high on the walls of York Minster. What the carving represents exactly is not quite clear, but I have interpreted it as a man being strangled by a monster or devil and I have adapted this theme to suit the pipe shape by having the arms of the monster coming from the man's own head. The smoker might pause to reflect on this when he lights up!

Figure 262

Figure 263

45   Chess Set

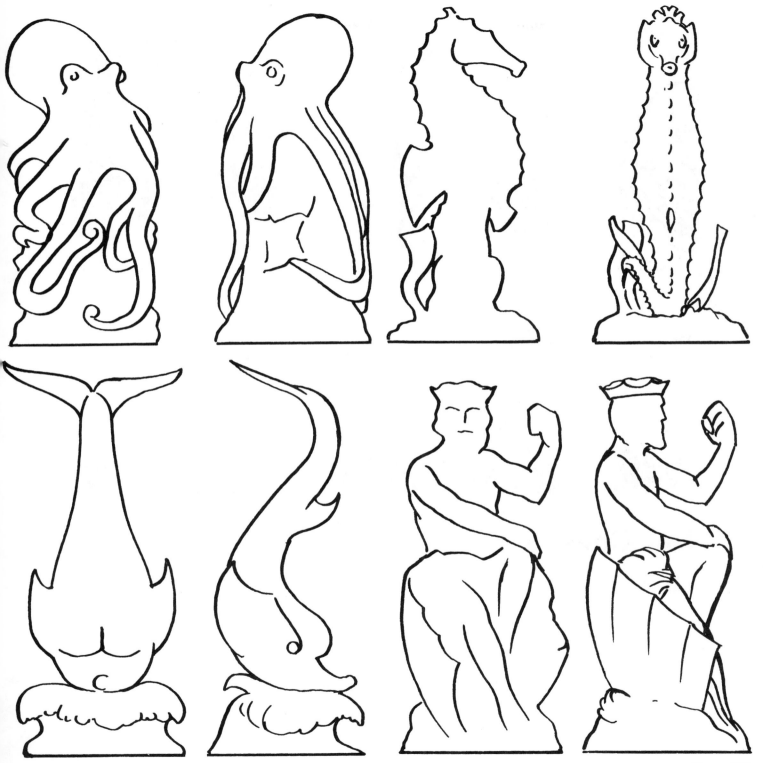

Figure 264

Figure 265

Designing the pieces of a chess set has almost as many potential variations as the game itself; added to this, a great many sets are used purely decoratively, while many others reflect the imagination of their owners or makers. The set under consideration here is one that was designed and made for an expert on marine life and three considerations governed the design: the suitability to the techniques of woodcarving; the relationship to the sea; and the mechanics of the game — so all pieces had to have a fairly solid top which could be comfortably handled by players.

King Neptune and the mermaid are purely symbolic; the dolphin is adapted from the traditional carved ones seen on furniture, and all the pawns are different species of fish — the perch illustrated was not in fact used because it is a freshwater species.

The sizes were planned from a 1½" (37mm) thick board of plum and branches of boxwood thick enough to convert to 1½" (37mm) square. Both are excellent for carving on this scale. There are no special problems in the carving. The smallest tool used is a 2mm No. 2. The scalloped effect on the seahorse may look very difficult but is simply a systematic progression of gouge cuts (see Fig. 271). The King's and Queen's tridents are made separately and inserted through drilled hands. It will be noticed that the pawns are based on the trout carving seen earlier in the book.

Figure 266 **Figure 267** **Figure 268**

Figure 269 **Figure 270** **Figure 271**

Figure 272

Figure 273

46   Bowl of Fruit

This is an easy carving, using up odd bits of timber very satisfactorily. Obviously the bowl of fruit will be further enhanced if it is made from a variety of attractive woods and could be made as and when offcuts presented themselves.

Try to find well-shaped items of fruit and vegetables – some specimens can be very smooth and bland, like Golden Delicious apples, whereas Bramleys are bulbous and deeply divided around the stalk.

It is desirable to have a piece of wood at least an inch or two longer than the finished fruit to allow it to be held in the vice.

Even the most inept draughtsman should be able to draw the apple, pear, or whatever; you could even cut it in half and trace around it, so it is easy enough to get the outline onto both sides of the blank. This can then be bandsawn. At this size a bow-saw or even a coping-saw could be used. The sawn shape can then be rounded off with a gouge, rasp or, as I used, a Stanley Surform. Leave an allowance for any details, such as the leaves at the end of the aubergine. These can then be cut in and shaped.

On most fruit the modelling is very simple, but more subtle than you might expect. Very careful sanding is required rather than clever carving and most of this can be done while the wood is held in the vice. When sanding is complete, except for the uncut end, saw the waste off. You can then hold the fruit carefully in the vice and finish the end.

A collection of these simple pieces in a bowl, well polished, looks quite striking, whilst single fruit can be used to make delightful gifts.

Figure 274

Figure 275

Figure 276

Figure 277

ABSTRACT FORMS

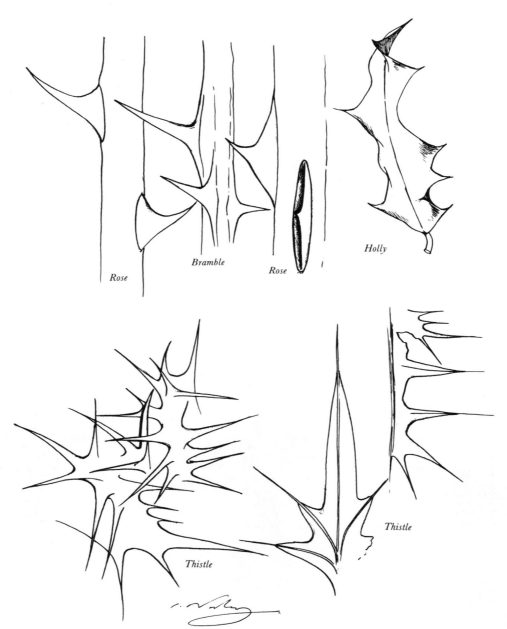

Rose

Bramble

Rose

Holly

Thistle

Thistle

Figure 278

47 Thorn

To the vast majority of the public, abstract art is something the Arts Council continually wastes their taxes on, and I would agree with them in the sense that much of modern art is a fraud. But all modern art cannot be grouped under the title "abstract", and much good abstract art can be appreciated by the most ardent traditionalist if he can try to understand it. "Abstract" means "to take away" and as I understand abstract art it is the act of "taking" a particular quality from an object or experience in the real world and portraying that quality in a visible medium in order to convey the artist's concept of that quality. The famous drawing of an apostle's praying hands by Durer conveys an idea to many people that a painting of the entire figure might well fail to do. In the same way, might not a suitably shaped piece of wood be able to convey the lightness and agility of a ballerina more intelligibly than a painstaking rendering of every visible detail?

I am not an abstract artist and my carving is merely a suggestion for a path that some people might like to follow. It is based on a rose thorn, the beautiful broken curves of the barb being repeated in every facet of the carving.

Mulberry wood carves very easily but it is not strong on short grain, such as the spikes, so care must be taken if you are using this wood. A spoon bent gouge is essential and the deeper the hollows the better. The great pleasure of carving abstract is that it is a relaxed, meditative occupation. There is no standard to work to, no level of accuracy to maintain and no real criticism, other than bad technique, to be levelled against it. You carve a bit and sit and study the effect; change a bit here and there as the fancy takes you, eliminating everything that does not contribute to the desired effect, and accentuating anything that does. The scope is endless.

Figure 279

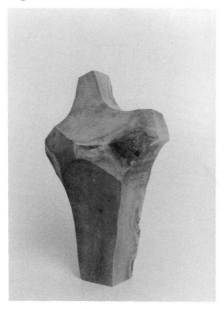

Figure 280

Figure 281

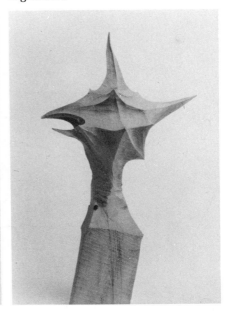

Figure 282

48 Village

Figure 283

Having been a painter of equestrian pictures for many years I also have a great interest in landscapes, and like most people, I am occasionally struck by the picturesque quality of a particular view. Since I no longer paint, but carve, I have spent many frustrating hours pondering the question of how landscape can be portrayed in three-dimensional sculpture. Undoubtedly, sculptors, on occasion, have strongly suggested an entire scene by the clever use of a single detail. I am reminded of a bronze entitled *cheetah* by Jonathan Kenworthy: it stands under a beobab tree, and with this suggestion of the African bush, as seen on films, one can share the cheetah's piercing gaze across the grasslands.

However, what I was more interested in was encapsulating the feel of a landscape in a recognisable form. Having studied the villages of the Cotswolds for many years, I tried to select the salient points that made these delightful spots typical. I felt that the enclosed atmosphere of the valleys they were invariably situated in was critical. There is a strong feeling of entering the valley, usually down a narrow winding lane, accompanied by a stream. The village appears as steep gables and dormers rising from clumps of trees. The church spire towers over the terraced row of workers' cottages. Ancient humpbacked bridges span the stream which disappears amongst old mill buildings. All around, softly-rounded hummocky hills scattered with copses and thickets, cut-off from the outside world, form deep cleavages that invite you to explore deeper into "Ruritania". Only the occasional scar of a quarry or an out-crop of rocks saves it from effeminate chocolate-box prettiness.

Sketches came next, just rough doodles, followed by an experiment with clay. See Fig. 284 Finally, I turned a large block of lime to a part of a sphere and carved my village.

The carving is quite straightforward, the buildings require the precision usually associated with dovetail joints. The spire of the church is added separately. The aesthetic considerations however, are endless. Halfway through I realised that one could use actual known skyline around the circumference by the subtle positioning of the component features; vistas could be created with depth and perspective. The carving could be used as a three-dimensional stage set.

I do not claim to have succeeded in this at all, but I think there is great potential to be explored.

Figure 284

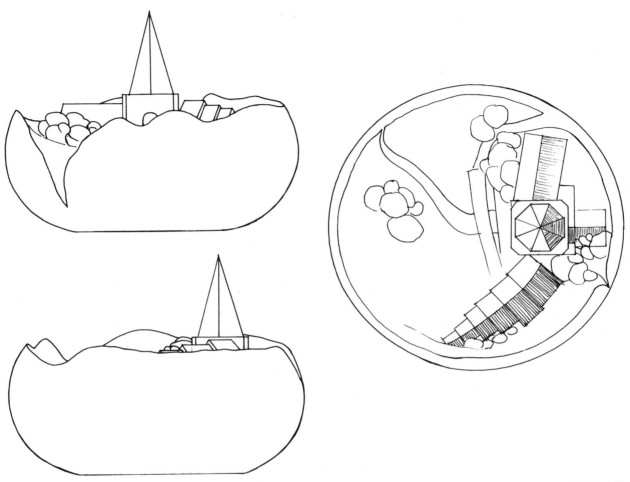

Figure 285

Figure 286

49 'Lily' Candle Holder

Figure 287

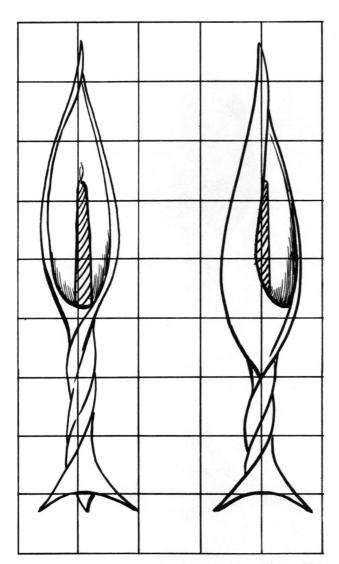

Figure 288

Plant forms have inspired so much art and design in such subtle and varied ways that to use it in such a basic manner as this candle holder seems absolutely naive, and yet the beautiful shape of the arum lily, both in its closed and open situations, presents so many practical adaptations, almost unchanged, that I felt it worthy of inclusion. Notice that in the drawings the design is more elongated, which after making the original, I felt would be preferable.

There are thousands of plant forms that could be used in similar ways and there are several books illustrating examples such as Prof. Karl Blossfeldt's *Art Forms in Nature*.

Using a log of wood about 5″ (125mm) in diameter of an unidentified species, I cut a flat surface on two sides and bandsawed the shape. Most of the rough shaping was done with a Surform and rasp on the outside and a rotary burr on the inside. The inside was carefully tooled, the outside filed and sanded, and the feet shaped with a knife. The whole process took less than an afternoon.

It is important to note that the candle has been lit for the purposes of photography only and in a design of this type it is essential that it is only used decoratively. If you wish to adapt the design to accept lighted candles ensure that the flame rises well clear of the wood.

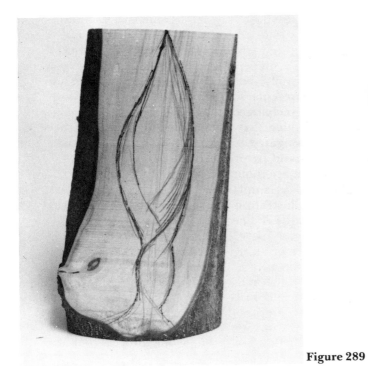

Figure 289

Figure 290

Figure 291

Figure 292

Figure 293

STUDENTS' WORK

One year after the publication of my first book *Techniques of Creative Woodcarving* I have realised that many beginners and potential beginners in the art of woodcarving feel that I am trying to teach them something which they do not have the ability to learn because that ability is congenital talent which you either have or don't have. I believe that anyone who has reasonable co-ordination, bodily control, strength and eyesight can learn to carve. To do so he must have tuition of some sort, be it teacher or book. That tuition should instruct him or her in the use of materials, tools and techniques in such a way as to make the work feasible. This being so, I believe success to be a measure of effort. Some of the beginners I have seen using useless wood, useless tools and little or no technique have my deepest sympathy and their "teachers" my lowest regard.

However, to show those who will say "fine, but I couldn't do it", that they could if they would care to try, I have included the work of a few students I have had over the last three years: a health education teacher, a cabinetmaking student, a carpenter, a retired engineer in the plastics industry, and my seven year old son. I don't think any of them would take kindly to the success of their efforts being written-off as "natural talent". It could be said that they had personal tuition, and no doubt that is preferable; however, they were taught by the same method outlined here and, more particularly, in the first book.

I fully recognise that using only a book will obviously be more difficult and many will have to learn some of the lessons the hard way, but with determination, perseverance and effort, success will follow.

1.   Miniature carvings by James Norbury (the author's son) aged 7

2. Head of Wagner carved in holly by Michael Price

3. Mediaeval Griffon carved from an old oak beam by Michael Price

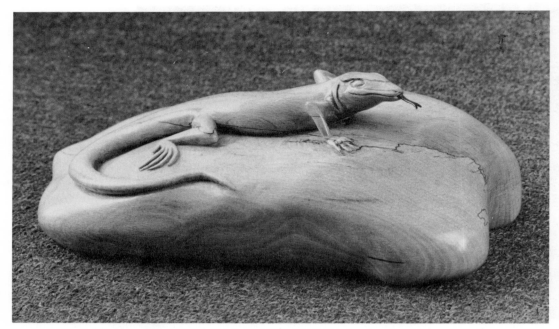

4. Lizard carved in spalted beech by David Johnson

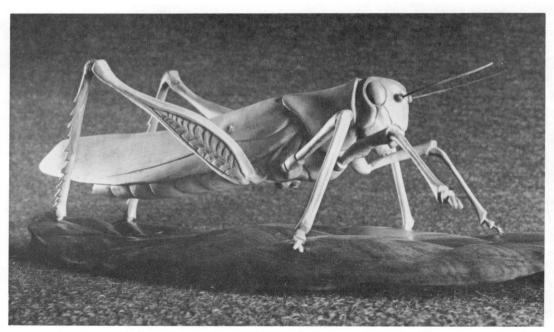

5. Locust carved in boxwood by David Johnson

6. & 7.   Pegusus carved in limewood by David Mansfield

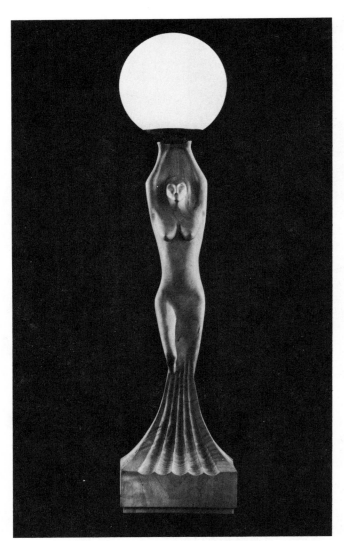

8. Lamp carved in cedar by Patrick Dunleavy

9. Welsh Dragon carved from an old oak beam by Patrick Dunleavy

10. The author, second left, teaching in Switzerland

11. Swiss students' work after five days. The author's original piece is far left and is a simplified version of the lugger falcon in the book.

Photographic Credits

The author wishes to thank the following for the use of their photographs.

Mr. R. Vanden Bosch for Figures 107 and 108 on page 77. Mr Roger Barrett and the Everyman Theatre, Cheltenham for Figures 133, 134 and 136 on pages 92 and 93.

NOTES

NOTES

NOTES

NOTES